Social Justice

Other Books of Related Interest:

At Issue Series

Are Government Bailouts Effective?

Are Unions Still Relevant?

The Occupy Movement

Should the Rich Pay Higher Taxes?

Current Controversies Series

Medicare

Poverty and Homelessness

Social Security

Introducing Issues with Opposing Viewpoints

Homelessness

Human Rights

Opposing Viewpoints Series

Civil Liberties

Criminal Justice

The Death Penalty

Multiracial America

GLOBALVIEWPOINTS

Social Justice

Noël Merino, Book Editor

GREENHAVEN PRESS

A part of Gale, Cengage Learning

GALE
CENGAGE Learning·

Farmington Hills, Mich • San Francisco • New York • Waterville, Maine
Meriden, Conn • Mason, Ohio • Chicago

Elizabeth Des Chenes, *Director, Content Strategy*
Cynthia Sanner, *Publisher*
Douglas Dentino, *Manager, New Product*

© 2014 Greenhaven Press, a part of Gale, Cengage Learning

WCN: 01-100-101

Gale and Greenhaven Press are registered trademarks used herein under license.

For more information, contact:
Greenhaven Press
27500 Drake Rd.
Farmington Hills, MI 48331-3535
Or you can visit our Internet site at gale.cengage.com

Articles in Greenhaven Press anthologies are often edited for length to meet page requirements. In addition, original titles of these works are changed to clearly present the main thesis and to explicitly indicate the author's opinion. Every effort is made to ensure that Greenhaven Press accurately reflects the original intent of the authors. Every effort has been made to trace the owners of copyrighted material.

Cover image copyright © infoart/Demotix/Corbis.

LIBRARY OF CONGRESS CATALOGING-IN-PUBLICATION DATA

Social justice (Greenhaven Press)
    Social justice / Noël Merino, book editor.
        pages cm. -- (Global viewpoints)
    Includes bibliographical references and index.
    ISBN 978-0-7377-6420-8 (hardcover) -- ISBN 978-0-7377-6421-5 (pbk.)
    1. Social justice. 2. Income distribution. I. Merino, Noël. II. Title.
    HM671.S6232 2014
    303.3'72--dc23
                                                    2013027891

Printed in Mexico
1 2 3 4 5 6 7 18 17 16 15 14

Contents

The increased unemployment caused by the global economic crisis, particularly among vulnerable groups, has worsened inequality and needs remedying.

Chapter 2: Social Justice and Minorities

Chapter 3: Social Justice and Gender

Foreword

*"The problems of all of humanity can
only be solved by all of humanity."*
   —Swiss author Friedrich Dürrenmatt

Global interdependence has become an undeniable reality. Mass media and technology have increased worldwide access to information and created a society of global citizens. Understanding and navigating this global community is a challenge, requiring a high degree of information literacy and a new level of learning sophistication.

Building on the success of its flagship series, Opposing Viewpoints, Greenhaven Press has created the Global Viewpoints series to examine a broad range of current, often controversial topics of worldwide importance from a variety of international perspectives. Providing students and other readers with the information they need to explore global connections and think critically about worldwide implications, each Global Viewpoints volume offers a panoramic view of a topic of widespread significance.

Drugs, famine, immigration—a broad, international treatment is essential to do justice to social, environmental, health, and political issues such as these. Junior high, high school, and early college students, as well as general readers, can all use Global Viewpoints anthologies to discern the complexities relating to each issue. Readers will be able to examine unique national perspectives while, at the same time, appreciating the interconnectedness that global priorities bring to all nations and cultures.

Material in each volume is selected from a diverse range of sources, including journals, magazines, newspapers, nonfiction books, speeches, government documents, pamphlets, organization newsletters, and position papers. Global Viewpoints is truly global, with material drawn primarily from international sources available in English and secondarily from US sources with extensive international coverage.

Features of each volume in the Global Viewpoints series include:

- An **annotated table of contents** that provides a brief summary of each essay in the volume, including the name of the country or area covered in the essay.

- An **introduction** specific to the volume topic.

- A **world map** to help readers locate the countries or areas covered in the essays.

- For each viewpoint, an **introduction** that contains notes about the author and source of the viewpoint explains why material from the specific country is being presented, summarizes the main points of the viewpoint, and offers three **guided reading questions** to aid in understanding and comprehension.

- **For further discussion** questions that promote critical thinking by asking the reader to compare and contrast aspects of the viewpoints or draw conclusions about perspectives and arguments.

- A worldwide list of **organizations to contact** for readers seeking additional information.

- A **periodical bibliography** for each chapter and a **bibliography of books** on the volume topic to aid in further research.

- A comprehensive **subject index** to offer access to people, places, events, and subjects cited in the text, with the countries covered in the viewpoints highlighted.

Global Viewpoints is designed for a broad spectrum of readers who want to learn more about current events, history, political science, government, international relations, economics, environmental science, world cultures, and sociology—students doing research for class assignments or debates, teachers and faculty seeking to supplement course materials, and others wanting to understand current issues better. By presenting how people in various countries perceive the root causes, current consequences, and proposed solutions to worldwide challenges, Global Viewpoints volumes offer readers opportunities to enhance their global awareness and their knowledge of cultures worldwide.

Introduction

*"All social values—liberty and opportu-
nity, income and wealth, and the bases
of self-respect—are to be distributed
equally unless an unequal distribution
of any, or all, of these values is to
everyone's advantage."*

—John Rawls,
A Theory of Justice

Social justice refers to the justice of social institutions where, to be just, each person is given what he or she is due, whether liberty, wealth, or some other social good. Economic goods are among the key social goods that impact individuals. One of the central components of assessing social justice among members of a community, a nation, or even on a global level involves assessment of the distribution of economic goods. Exactly what makes economic distribution just, however, is subject to wide disagreement, and some have argued that the entire concept of social justice is suspect because of incoherence in the very notion of just economic distribution. One key difference among the competing theories of just economic distribution is the way in which equality is understood.

One theory of just economic distribution is that of economic egalitarianism; that is, where equality of economic outcomes are created for all members of society. German philosophers Karl Marx and Friedrich Engels can be seen as advocating a version of economic egalitarianism. In their view, differences in income and class are signs of social injustice, and the goal is to remove all class differences and the use of money by the adoption of communism. Modern theories of socialism advocate economic egalitarianism within an economic system of social ownership, thus removing inequalities.

The achievement of economic egalitarianism in a socialist society that uses money must be achieved by some kind of government redistribution, such as through taxation, in order to achieve equality of economic outcomes. Economic egalitarianism takes equality of economic outcomes to be a sign of just economic distribution. However, equality of outcomes is not the only interpretation of equality for the purposes of assessing the justice of economic distribution.

The American philosopher John Rawls developed a theory of social justice that views just economic distribution as a result of fairness and equality of opportunity. Rawls posits that each person in a society has an equal right to basic economic goods; however, justice does not necessarily demand that beyond these basic goods there be no economic inequalities. When economic inequalities do exist—such as differences in incomes and wealth—Rawls claims that they are just if two conditions are met: 1) that economic inequalities are tied to positions that are open to all under conditions of fair equality of opportunity, and 2) that economic inequalities are of greatest benefit to the least advantaged. For example, it may be just for a business owner to receive a salary that is ten times larger than the poorest member of society if the business owner's position is open to all members of society through fair equality of opportunity, and if paying the high salary improves the economic condition of the poorest members of society, perhaps by creating the incentive for the business owner to expand business that results in increased wages and more jobs.

For Rawls, economic inequalities in society do not violate justice when they make things better for those who are worse off. In Rawls's view, a society of economic egalitarianism where each person has equal income may not actually be the most just society: Economic wealth overall may be lowered by this kind of equality. Allowing unequal incomes may actually raise overall wealth so that even the poorest member of society in this scheme is better off than in a society with equal economic incomes. What is ultimately most important for social justice for Rawls is equality of opportunity, not sameness of outcomes.

Austrian-born British economist Friedrich Hayek denies that there is any such thing as social justice. A proponent of the free market, Hayek claims that the economic outcomes of the market cannot be called just or unjust. For Hayek, any attempt to interfere with the outcomes of the market—by redistributing income through taxes, for example—is contrary to a free society and violates individual liberty. The only important understanding of equality in this view is equality under the law protective of liberty. For Hayek and other opponents of social justice, any attempt to rein in the free market by attempting to engineer economic outcomes or economic opportunities is itself an injustice, violating the liberty of individuals. Thus, to posit the notion of social justice contingent on assessing the justice of economic distribution is already suspect by assuming that intervention is a just possibility.

One component of social justice is just economic distribution, but questions of how this should be defined and how this ought to be achieved have no easy answers. Is economic inequality, in income or in wealth, always a sign of injustice? What if economic inequality falls along racial lines or according to gender? Should countries enact policies to avoid extreme income inequality? How should the value of liberty be balanced against the value of equality? Is economic inequality among countries a sign of global injustice? If so, how should it be remedied? Varying viewpoints that attempt to answer these questions and others related to issues of social justice, both within countries and among countries, are explored in *Global Viewpoints: Social Justice*.

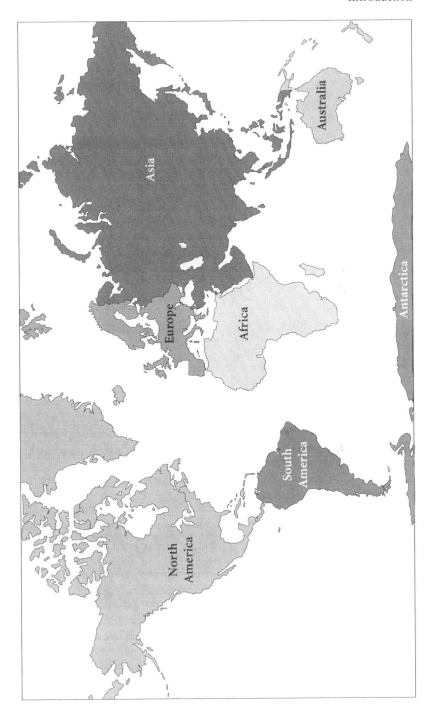

GLOBALVIEWPOINTS

Social Justice and Economic Inequality

Economic Inequality in the United States Has Grown Dangerously Unjust

Joseph E. Stiglitz

In the following viewpoint, Joseph E. Stiglitz argues that wealth in America has become overly concentrated in the top 1 percent. Stiglitz contends that the growth in wealth of the rich, along with a decrease in wealth of the middle class, has caused severe inequality that has several negative effects. He claims that the rich have influenced policy to such a degree that the inequality is now self-perpetuating and threatens to result in social unrest. Stiglitz is an economist, professor at Columbia University, and author of The Price of Inequality: How Today's Divided Society Endangers Our Future.

As you read, consider the following questions:

1. Stiglitz claims that the top 1 percent has seen their incomes rise by what percentage over the past decade?

2. What does the author say is the most obvious example of a policy created by the top 1 percent for the top 1 percent?

3. What fraction of Americans is on food stamps, according to the author?

Joseph E. Stiglitz, "Of the 1%, by the 1%, for the 1%," *Vanity Fair*, vol. 53, no. 5, May 2011, p. 126. Reproduced by permission.

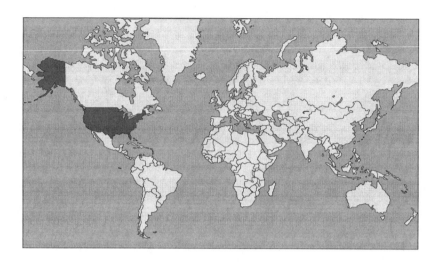

It's no use pretending that what has obviously happened has not in fact happened. The upper 1 percent of Americans are now taking in nearly a quarter of the nation's income every year. In terms of wealth rather than income, the top 1 percent control 40 percent. Their lot in life has improved considerably. Twenty-five years ago, the corresponding figures were 12 percent and 33 percent. One response might be to celebrate the ingenuity and drive that brought good fortune to these people, and to contend that a rising tide lifts all boats. That response would be misguided. While the top 1 percent have seen their incomes rise 18 percent over the past decade, those in the middle have actually seen their incomes fall. For men with only high school degrees, the decline has been precipitous—12 percent in the last quarter century alone. All the growth in recent decades—and more—has gone to those at the top. In terms of income equality, America lags behind any country in the old, ossified Europe that President George W. Bush used to deride. Among our closest counterparts are Russia with its oligarchs and Iran. While many of the old centers of inequality in Latin America, such as Brazil, have been striving in recent years, rather successfully, to improve the plight of the poor and reduce gaps in income, America has allowed inequality to grow.

Economists long ago tried to justify the vast inequalities that seemed so troubling in the mid-19th century—inequalities that are but a pale shadow of what we are seeing in America today. The justification they came up with was called "marginal-productivity theory." In a nutshell, this theory associated higher incomes with higher productivity and a greater contribution to society. It is a theory that has always been cherished by the rich. Evidence for its validity, however, remains thin. The corporate executives who helped bring on the recession of the past three years [2008–2011]—whose contribution to our society, and to their own companies, has been massively negative—went on to receive large bonuses. In some cases, companies were so embarrassed about calling such rewards "performance bonuses" that they felt compelled to change the name to "retention bonuses" (even if the only thing being retained was bad performance). Those who have contributed great positive innovations to our society, from the pioneers of genetic understanding to the pioneers of the Information Age, have received a pittance compared with those responsible for the financial innovations that brought our global economy to the brink of ruin.

All the growth in recent decades—and more—has gone to those at the top.

The Problem with Inequality

Some people look at income inequality and shrug their shoulders. So what if this person gains and that person loses? What matters, they argue, is not how the pie is divided but the size of the pie. That argument is fundamentally wrong. An economy in which *most* citizens are doing worse year after year—an economy like America's—is not likely to do well over the long haul. There are several reasons for this.

First, growing inequality is the flip side of something else: shrinking opportunity. Whenever we diminish equality of opportunity, it means that we are not using some of our most valuable assets—our people—in the most productive way possible. Second, many of the distortions that lead to inequality—such as those associated with monopoly power and preferential tax treatment for special interests—undermine the efficiency of the economy. This new inequality goes on to create new distortions, undermining efficiency even further. To give just one example, far too many of our most talented young people, seeing the astronomical rewards, have gone into finance rather than into fields that would lead to a more productive and healthy economy.

Third, and perhaps most important, a modern economy requires "collective action"—it needs government to invest in infrastructure, education, and technology. The United States and the world have benefited greatly from government-sponsored research that led to the Internet, to advances in public health, and so on. But America has long suffered from an underinvestment in infrastructure (look at the condition of our highways and bridges, our railroads and airports), in basic research, and in education at all levels. Further cutbacks in these areas lie ahead.

None of this should come as a surprise—it is simply what happens when a society's wealth distribution becomes lopsided. The more divided a society becomes in terms of wealth, the more reluctant the wealthy become to spend money on common needs. The rich don't need to rely on government for parks or education or medical care or personal security—they can buy all these things for themselves. In the process, they become more distant from ordinary people, losing whatever empathy they may once have had. They also worry about strong government—one that could use its powers to adjust the balance, take some of their wealth, and invest it for the common good. The top 1 percent may complain about the kind of government we have in America, but in truth they like it just fine: too gridlocked to redistribute, too divided to do anything but lower taxes.

Law and Policy Built for the Rich

Economists are not sure how to fully explain the growing inequality in America. The ordinary dynamics of supply and demand have certainly played a role: Labor-saving technologies have reduced the demand for many "good" middle-class, blue-collar jobs. Globalization has created a worldwide marketplace, pitting expensive unskilled workers in America against cheap unskilled workers overseas. Social changes have also played a role—for instance, the decline of unions, which once represented a third of American workers and now represent about 12 percent.

The more divided a society becomes in terms of wealth, the more reluctant the wealthy become to spend money on common needs.

But one big part of the reason we have so much inequality is that the top 1 percent want it that way. The most obvious example involves tax policy. Lowering tax rates on capital gains, which is how the rich receive a large portion of their income, has given the wealthiest Americans close to a free ride. Monopolies and near monopolies have always been a source of economic power—from John D. Rockefeller at the beginning of the last century to Bill Gates at the end. Lax enforcement of antitrust laws, especially during Republican administrations, has been a godsend to the top 1 percent. Much of today's inequality is due to manipulation of the financial system, enabled by changes in the rules that have been bought and paid for by the financial industry itself—one of its best investments ever. The government lent money to financial institutions at close to 0 percent interest and provided generous bailouts on favorable terms when all else failed. Regulators turned a blind eye to a lack of transparency and to conflicts of interest.

"The One Percent," cartoon by RJ Matson and Cagle Cartoons. Copyright © 2011 by RJ Matson and Cagle Cartoons.

A Self-Perpetuating System

When you look at the sheer volume of wealth controlled by the top 1 percent in this country, it's tempting to see our growing inequality as a quintessentially American achievement—we started way behind the pack, but now we're doing inequality on a world-class level. And it looks as if we'll be building on this achievement for years to come, because what made it possible is self-reinforcing. Wealth begets power, which begets more wealth. During the savings-and-loan scandal of the 1980s—a scandal whose dimensions, by today's standards, seem almost quaint—the banker Charles Keating was asked by a congressional committee whether the $1.5 million he had spread among a few key elected officials could actually buy influence. "I certainly hope so," he replied. The Supreme Court, in its recent *Citizens United* [*v. Federal Election Commission* (2010)] case, has enshrined the right of corporations to buy government, by removing limitations on campaign spending.

The personal and the political are today in perfect alignment. Virtually all U.S. senators, and most of the representatives in the House, are members of the top 1 percent when they arrive, are kept in office by money from the top 1 percent, and know that if they serve the top 1 percent well they will be rewarded by the top 1 percent when they leave office. By and large, the key executive-branch policy makers on trade and economic policy also come from the top 1 percent. When pharmaceutical companies receive a trillion-dollar gift—through legislation prohibiting the government, the largest buyer of drugs, from bargaining over price—it should not come as cause for wonder. It should not make jaws drop that a tax bill cannot emerge from Congress unless big tax cuts are put in place for the wealthy. Given the power of the top 1 percent, this is the way you would *expect* the system to work.

America's inequality distorts our society in every conceivable way. There is, for one thing, a well-documented lifestyle effect—people outside the top 1 percent increasingly live beyond their means. Trickle-down economics may be a chimera, but trickle-down behaviorism is very real. Inequality massively distorts our foreign policy. The top 1 percent rarely serve in the military—the reality is that the "all-volunteer" army does not pay enough to attract their sons and daughters, and patriotism goes only so far. Plus, the wealthiest class feels no pinch from higher taxes when the nation goes to war: Borrowed money will pay for all that. Foreign policy, by definition, is about the balancing of national interests and national resources. With the top 1 percent in charge, and paying no price, the notion of balance and restraint goes out the window. There is no limit to the adventures we can undertake; corporations and contractors stand only to gain. The rules of economic globalization are likewise designed to benefit the rich: They encourage competition among countries for *business*, which drives down taxes on corporations, weakens health and environmental protections, and undermines what used to

25

be viewed as the "core" labor rights, which include the right to collective bargaining. Imagine what the world might look like if the rules were designed instead to encourage competition among countries for *workers*. Governments would compete in providing economic security, low taxes on ordinary wage earners, good education, and a clean environment—things workers care about. But the top 1 percent don't need to care.

America's inequality distorts our society in every conceivable way.

The Danger of Inequality

Or, more accurately, they think they don't [need to care]. Of all the costs imposed on our society by the top 1 percent, perhaps the greatest is this: the erosion of our sense of identity, in which fair play, equality of opportunity, and a sense of community are so important. America has long prided itself on being a fair society, where everyone has an equal chance of getting ahead, but the statistics suggest otherwise: The chances of a poor citizen, or even a middle-class citizen, making it to the top in America are smaller than in many countries of Europe. The cards are stacked against them. It is this sense of an unjust system without opportunity that has given rise to the conflagrations in the Middle East: Rising food prices and growing and persistent youth unemployment simply served as kindling. With youth unemployment in America at around 20 percent (and in some locations, and among some socio-demographic groups, at twice that); with one out of six Americans desiring a full-time job not able to get one; with one out of seven Americans on food stamps (and about the same number suffering from "food insecurity")—given all this, there is ample evidence that something has blocked the vaunted "trickling down" from the top 1 percent to everyone else. All of this is having the predictable effect of creating alienation—voter turnout among those in their 20s in the last election stood at 21 percent, comparable to the unemployment rate.

In recent weeks [spring 2011] we have watched people taking to the streets by the millions to protest political, economic, and social conditions in the oppressive societies they inhabit. Governments have been toppled in Egypt and Tunisia. Protests have erupted in Libya, Yemen, and Bahrain. The ruling families elsewhere in the region look on nervously from their air-conditioned penthouses—will they be next? They are right to worry. These are societies where a minuscule fraction of the population—less than 1 percent—controls the lion's share of the wealth; where wealth is a main determinant of power; where entrenched corruption of one sort or another is a way of life; and where the wealthiest often stand actively in the way of policies that would improve life for people in general.

As we gaze out at the popular fervor in the streets, one question to ask ourselves is this: When will it come to America? In important ways, our own country has become like one of these distant, troubled places.

A Narrow View of Self-Interest

Alexis de Tocqueville once described what he saw as a chief part of the peculiar genius of American society—something he called "self-interest properly understood." The last two words were the key. Everyone possesses self-interest in a narrow sense: I want what's good for me right now! Self-interest "properly understood" is different. It means appreciating that paying attention to everyone else's self-interest—in other words, the common welfare—is in fact a precondition for one's own ultimate well-being. Tocqueville was not suggesting that there was anything noble or idealistic about this outlook—in fact, he was suggesting the opposite. It was a mark of American pragmatism. Those canny Americans understood a basic fact: Looking out for the other guy isn't just good for the soul—it's good for business.

America has long prided itself on being a fair society, where everyone has an equal chance of getting ahead, but the statistics suggest otherwise.

The top 1 percent have the best houses, the best educations, the best doctors, and the best lifestyles, but there is one thing that money doesn't seem to have bought: an understanding that their fate is bound up with how the other 99 percent live. Throughout history, this is something that the top 1 percent eventually do learn. Too late.

Economic Growth in India and China Has Exacerbated Inequality

Deepankar Basu

In the following viewpoint, edited by Cengage Learning, Deepankar Basu argues that by using a measurement of inequality that is based on non-income dimensions of health and education rather than solely on income or wealth, data show that both India and China have had rapid economic growth in recent decades that has significantly increased socioeconomic inequality. Basu claims that at fault is the neoliberal policy making that is biased against the poor. Basu is an assistant professor of economics at the University of Massachusetts Amherst.

As you read, consider the following questions:

1. According to the author, which six countries stand out as notable examples of countries with neoliberal economic policies and increased socioeconomic inequality since 1990?
2. Which seven countries show the largest declines in socioeconomic inequality, according to the author?
3. Which of India's neighboring countries show strong evidence of improvement in socioeconomic inequality over the last two decades, according to Basu?

Deepankar Basu, "Socio-economic Inequality in India and the World Since 1990," *Sanhati*, November 17, 2011. Edited by Cengage Learning. Reproduced by permission.

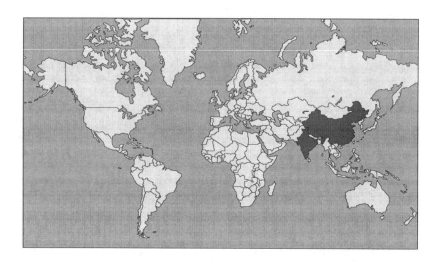

Socio-economic inequality refers to a broad measure of inequality. It tries to capture societal inequality along both income (and wealth) and non-income dimensions. Why should we look at the broader measure of socio-economic inequality? This is because traditional measures that focus exclusively on income (or wealth) inequality capture only a narrow slice of socio-economic inequality since, by construction, they leave out non-income dimensions of well-being like mortality, incidence and burden of common diseases, nutrition, educational attainment and social status deriving from factors like caste, race or ethnicity.

Indirect Measures of Socio-Economic Inequality

While constructing direct measures of socio-economic inequality is a daunting task because of data problems, it is possible to come up with *indirect measures* of socio-economic inequality. Recent research that I have undertaken in this area has proposed an intuitive and simple-to-compute indirect measure for tracking changes in socio-economic inequality over time by using the variation in life expectancy at birth (LEB) across countries. Using this measure we see very vividly that countries which aggressively adopted neoliberal economic policies have witnessed sharp deterioration in socio-economic inequality since 1990. Notable examples of such countries are India, China, Kenya, Thailand, Ghana and Chad. This corroborates the concerns of the critics of neoliberalism who have pointed out, over and over again, that the growth process of the past few decades has been massively disequalizing.

There are at least three reasons that make this indirect measure useful for activists, researchers and policy makers. First, there is a big problem of unavailability of income distribution data for much of the developing world. For instance, between 1990 and 2009, income distribution data was available in the World Development Indicators (the most comprehensive online database on the developing world maintained by the World Bank) between a maximum of 25 percent of countries in 2000, and a minimum of 6 percent of the countries in 1990. Thus, even in the best case scenario, about 75 percent of developing countries do have income distribution data available.

Countries which aggressively adopted neoliberal economic policies have witnessed sharp deterioration in socio-economic inequality since 1990.

Second, when data on income or consumption expenditure distribution is available for developing countries its quality is often low and [it is] beset with well-known problems. Changes in definitions or survey methodology often make comparability over time difficult. It is also well understood that household surveys, the source of income distribution data, suffer from the problems of under-reporting and under-coverage of the richer sections of the population. Even when reliable data on income distribution is obtained, it is not easy to convert that to measures of aggregate inequality like the Gini coefficient [a measure of statistical dispersion].

Third, data on the distribution of non-income measures of well-being are even more difficult to come by. But can we even come up with a simple measure of the distribution of the non-income aspects of well-being across the population? Recent research suggests that we can. The idea is the following: While it is difficult to capture *all* non-income aspects of inequality in one simple measure, life expectancy at birth (LEB) has been proposed by social scientists as a broad social indicator of social well-being that captures many of the important dimensions of living standards that are left out by pure income measures. . . .

The Components of Improved LEB

The construction of the indirect measure of socio-economic inequality starts from the fairly intuitive idea that improvements in LEB (and possibly other indicators of living standard as well) over time for any country can be decomposed into three parts. The first part arises due to increases in per capita income over time, which allows families, on average, to eat better and more nutritious food, live in better houses with better sanitation facilities, purchase better and more effective medical care, etc.

The second part comes from improvements in, and diffusion of, medical technology. This is primarily driven by improvements in, and diffusion of, medical technology that reduces the impact of diseases on the general health of human populations. Improvements in pre- and post-natal care, access to hospitals (or medical professionals) for childbirth, and availability of generic drugs for dealing with common diseases like diarrhea, malaria, TB [tuberculosis] and AIDS can have an enormous positive impact on LEB.

The third part can be attributed to the whole complex sets of factors (institutions of governance, public policy stance, effectiveness of public provisioning, status of disadvantaged groups like women and other minorities, etc.) that *distribute* income growth and access to medical technology across various sections of society. What is the rationale for this assertion? It is the following intuitive idea: Once income growth and improvements in medical technology (and other relevant exogenous factors like HIV prevalence) *have been accounted for*, improvements in LEB are bound to be positively impacted by redistribution towards the poor (broadly defined to include access to public goods like education and health care); on the other hand, redistribution away from the poor, i.e. [that is], increases in societal inequality, would have negative impacts on improvements in living standards.

The Performance of Comparable Countries

This immediately suggests a method for constructing an indirect measure of socio-economic inequality. To do so, roughly, we compute the average improvement in LEB for countries which have witnessed similar growth of per capita income and have had similar access to medical technology taking account of the fact that the relationship between LEB and per capita income is nonlinear (i.e., we allow for the fact that the marginal improvement in LEB for each unit of real per capita income increase tapers off as per capita income levels rise).

> *High growth which is accompanied by worsening inequality . . . reduces the positive impact of income growth on living standards, especially of the poor.*

Next we divide the countries into two groups: those that performed better and those that performed worse than average. This division gives us some important information: All those countries which recorded a better-than-average improvement in LEB must have done so because of a progressive redistribution; all those countries which performed worse than average must have witnessed a regressive redistribution, where redistribution includes both income and non-income dimensions of well-being.

Thus, we arrive at our indirect measure of socio-economic inequality: *changes in how much a country under or over performed the average improvement in LEB over a period of time is a quantitative measure of the change in socio-economic inequality during that period. A positive value of the measure suggests a decrease and a negative value suggests an increase of socio-economic inequality over the relevant period.*

Before we look at how countries have performed in terms of our indirect measure of socio-economic inequality, let us note an important implication of this methodology. The construction and use of the indirect measure proposed here highlight the important but oft-neglected point that as much as, or probably more than, economic growth itself the nature of that growth matters. High growth which is accompanied by worsening inequality (and reduced access of the poor to public goods) reduces the positive impact of income growth on living standards, especially of the poor. Conversely, even low economic growth that is more equitably distributed can have a significantly large impact on the material conditions of the poor. This means that the growth fetish currently gripping Indian policy circles is not only diversionary, it is patently misleading.

The Comparison of Countries

How do countries of the world perform in terms of changes in socio-economic inequality during the last two decades? Which countries show large declines and which show large increases in socio-economic inequality? . . . Among the countries which display the largest declines in socio-economic inequality, according to my measure, are Rwanda, Botswana, Gabon, Niger, Nepal, Guatemala, and Bangladesh. On the other end of the scale, some of the countries which displayed the largest in-

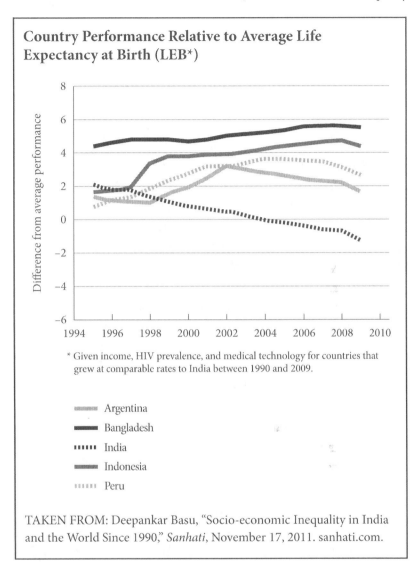

Country Performance Relative to Average Life Expectancy at Birth (LEB*)

* Given income, HIV prevalence, and medical technology for countries that grew at comparable rates to India between 1990 and 2009.

Argentina
Bangladesh
India
Indonesia
Peru

TAKEN FROM: Deepankar Basu, "Socio-economic Inequality in India and the World Since 1990," *Sanhati*, November 17, 2011. sanhati.com.

creases in socio-economic inequality are China, Republic of [the] Congo, Chad, Thailand, India, and Kenya.

Two countries which have grown very rapidly since the 1990s but have not managed to translate that rapid economic growth into improvements in LEB are China and India. Both countries figure towards the very end of the list of rankings; India is ranked 88 and China 98 among 98 countries for whom the ranking was computed. This indicates that the growth process under way in both countries must have increased socio-economic inequality significantly.

It might be thought that the improvement metric is biased against countries that have registered high growth. This is not the case for two reasons. First, the comparison is made, at each point in time, between countries that have similar per capita income; hence all countries with similar levels of per capita income are treated in the same way. Second, as indicated above, the income-LEB relationship takes into account the inherent nonlinearity involved. Thus, the improvement metric already accounts for the fact that marginal increases in LEB calls for higher income growth as LEB increases.

The fact that the metric is not biased against high-growth countries can also be seen from the rankings themselves. Countries with relatively high growth rates which also have shown rapid improvement in socio-economic inequality are Bhutan, Bangladesh, Mozambique, and South Africa. This is in stark contrast to high-growth countries with large increases in socio-economic inequality like China, India, and Thailand. On the other side, there are countries which had low growth in real per capita income and also witnessed increases in socio-economic inequality. Examples of such countries are Central African Republic, Kenya, and Zambia. . . .

Two countries which have grown very rapidly since the 1990s but have not managed to translate that rapid economic growth into improvements in LEB are China and India.

India and Its Neighbours

How does India compare with its neighbours?. . .

While Nepal and Bangladesh give strong evidence of improvement in socio-economic inequality and access of the poor to basic public goods, Pakistan shows stagnation and Sri Lanka shows worsening over this period though it remains an above-average performer. Bhutan has been a below-average performer all through the period, though its distance from average performance has been declining over time; that indicates some improvement over time.

The big exception is India which shows not only a steady worsening of socio-economic inequality but a switch from an above to a below average performer country. A more detailed historical and institutional analysis of each of these South Asian countries needs to be taken up to understand the reasons behind this divergence. While such an analysis will be taken up in future research, it seems safe to conclude from this evidence ... that the effects of rapid economic growth since the 1990s have not percolated down to the poorer sections of Indian society. In fact, it seems to have worsened socio-economic inequality and curtailed access of the poor to essential public goods like health care and education.

The growth process currently under way in India (and China) is inherently biased against the poor, the marginalized and underprivileged.

The Problem with Neoliberalism

Critics of the neoliberal turn to policy making in India, and the world in general, since the mid-1980s have pointed out that the growth process under a neoliberal regime is inherently anti-poor. Most of the dividends of economic growth is cornered by the already well-off. In parallel with an inegalitarian growth process, neoliberalism also whittles down whatever welfare state measures might have been in place before its adoption. Inegalitarian growth and erosion of state-assisted welfare provisioning increase socio-economic inequality drastically. Drawing on some recent research, this [viewpoint] has provided empirical evidence in support of such a view.

Two comparison groups provide a powerful and disturbing insight into India's growth process. First, there are many countries which have grown at rates very similar to India's but which have managed to register marked declines in socio-economic inequalities (as captured by the measure discussed in this [viewpoint]). In stark contrast to this, India has witnessed an increase in socio-economic inequality since 1990. Second, in comparison to its close neighbours, with whom India has many geographical, climactic, cultural and social commonalities, India emerges as the worst performer among the South Asian countries.

The implications of this finding are straightforward. The growth process currently under way in India (and China) is inherently biased against the poor, the marginalized and underprivileged. If economic growth is to lead to substantial improvements in the living standards (measured by indicators of well-being like life expectancy, literacy, infant mortality) of the vast majority of the world's population, a radically different socio-economic paradigm must be put in place of the currently dominant neoliberal one.

In Africa, Widespread Poverty and Income Inequalities Need to Be Addressed

Maurice Mubila, Laurence Lannes, and Mohamed S. Ben Aissa

In the following viewpoint, Maurice Mubila, Laurence Lannes, and Mohamed S. Ben Aissa contend that in recent decades poverty in Africa has increased, as has income inequality. The authors claim that the rate of poverty and severity of inequality varies on the continent, but they argue that even in high-growth countries, poverty and inequality are problems. They conclude that a new strategy of inclusive growth must be implemented. Mubila is chief statistician and Lannes is principal health economist at the African Development Bank. Aissa is professor of economics at the University of Tunis and consultant to the African Development Bank.

As you read, consider the following questions:

1. According to the authors, in what five African countries does poverty among young people exceed 80 percent?
2. The poor class in Africa holds what percentage of income, according to the authors?

Maurice Mubila, Laurence Lannes, and Mohamed S. Ben Aissa, "Briefing Note 5: Income Inequality in Africa," African Development Bank Group, March 7, 2012. www.afdb.org. Reproduced by permission.

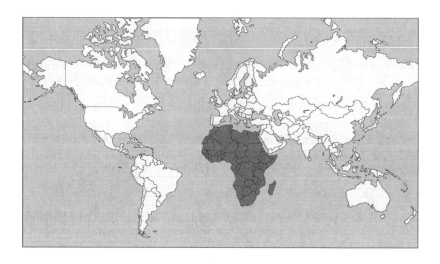

3. To combat inequality, the authors suggest policies that will help create more people in what class?

This [viewpoint] examines the problem of income inequality in Africa. Specifically, it addresses its trend and variations as well as the role of the African Development Bank in tackling it. Africa accounts for a large share of the world's people living in absolute poverty. Its share of the world's poor rose from just below 20% to close to 25%. Nearly 50% of the population in sub-Saharan Africa lives on less than US $1 a day today: the world's highest rate of extreme poverty in the world.

Growth and Poverty in Africa

The number of impoverished people has doubled since 1981. Since the late 1980s, the number of people living on less than US $1 per day in sub-Saharan Africa rose by 70 million, reaching 290 million in 1998, which is over 46% of the total population. In Liberia, nearly 60% of the population lives on less than US $2 a day. In the Central African Republic, the figure is 50%. By contrast, in North Africa, only 2.2% of the population lives on less than US $1 a day, and 23% on less than US $2.

Growth has not entirely eluded Africa. In the 2000s, six of the world's ten fastest-growth countries were in Africa, but this has not significantly helped to equal incomes or to redistribute wealth. Accelerated per capita growth has failed to create enough job opportunities for the young, who comprise the majority of the poor, of whom young women and rural youth are the poorest. Whereas an average of 72% of the youth population in Africa lives with less than US $2 per day, in Nigeria, Ethiopia, Uganda, Zambia and Burundi, the incidence of poverty among young people stands at over 80%.

In addition to being [one] of the poorest regions in the world, Africa is also the world's second most inequitable region after Latin America.

In resource-poor countries suffering from net trade losses due to higher import prices for food and energy, growth in per capita income is too low. Further, in resource-rich countries—Congo, Nigeria, Angola and South Africa—that benefit from net trade gains such that their real income increases faster than real output, performance has also been poor.

Income Inequality in Africa

In addition to being [one] of the poorest regions in the world, Africa is also the world's second most inequitable region after Latin America. Inequalities have not diminished over time. In 2010, six out of the 10 most unequal countries worldwide were in sub-Saharan Africa, and more specifically in southern Africa.

In all African countries, the richest capture the largest share of income. When measured by the share of income that goes to the poorest, inequalities are striking, and accompanied by geographic disparities between urban and rural areas where the poor are concentrated. In Mozambique, the mean share of the lowest 20% of the population is 5.2% of total income while the top 20% has a share of 51.5%. A larger percentage of the population is poor in rural areas (56.9%), compared to urban areas (49.6%).

The poor (<$2/day) account for 60.8% of Africa's population and hold 36.5% of total income in Africa. The rich (>$20/day) account for 4.8% of the population and 18.8% of total income. These disparities are reabsorbed by the middle class in terms of embodying the concept of equity in income distribution. For example, the lower-middle class ($4–$10/day) is almost balanced: 8.7% of the population lives on $4 to $10 per day and accounts for 9.9% of total income. It appears that income distribution in Africa is characterized by some equity for the middle-income classes and significant differences within the rich and poor income groups.

Recent impressive growth has not improved widespread poverty or income inequalities that continue to prevail across the continent.

Overall, southern Africa is the most unequal part of Africa. Namibia, Comoros, South Africa, Angola, Botswana, Lesotho and Swaziland count among the continent's top ten most unequal countries and the most striking increase in inequality is found in South Africa and the Central African Republic whose Gini coefficients have risen from 58 to 67 between 2000–2006 and from 43 to 56 between 2003–2008, respectively.

The Need for Inclusive Growth

As the bank defines its new long-term strategy, it is an opportune moment to support inclusive growth that can translate into wider participation in the growth process and less income inequality. The Arab Spring [referring to revolutionary protests in the Arab world beginning in December 2008] and

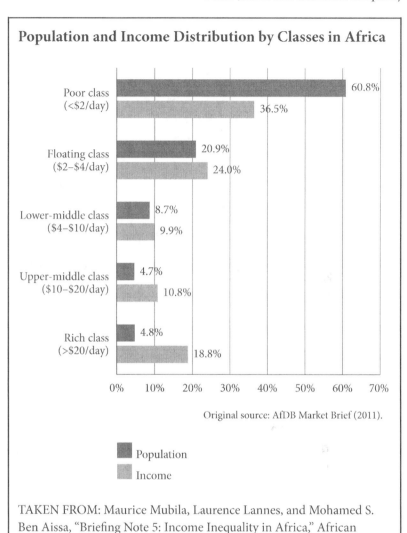

Population and Income Distribution by Classes in Africa

Original source: AfDB Market Brief (2011).

TAKEN FROM: Maurice Mubila, Laurence Lannes, and Mohamed S. Ben Aissa, "Briefing Note 5: Income Inequality in Africa," African Development Bank Group, March 7, 2012. www.afdb.org.

growing inequalities in southern Africa have put into stark relief the urgency of such an agenda.

The bank's new human development strategy argues that income inequalities must be addressed by more inclusive growth that increases employment opportunities for all, yields productivity gains and economic growth, and provides a sense of dignity and control over personal destiny. This strategy seeks to achieve value for money and accountability in service delivery by fighting corruption and promoting voice in decision making. It seeks greater inclusion and social cohesion thanks to stronger safety nets and other risk protection mechanisms. This inclusive growth agenda will be included in the bank's long-term strategy to draw the attention of regional member countries to the need to take action to promote a more equal distribution of income and wealth.

Recent impressive growth has not improved widespread poverty or income inequalities that continue to prevail across the continent. The existence of a strong middle class accompanied by the right polices may help reduce income inequalities. If this is the case, those government policies and donor interventions that help create a middle class will have the effect of lowering income inequalities and hence poverty levels.

Latin America Has Made Progress in Reducing Its Extreme Inequality

Mark Loyka

In the following viewpoint, Mark Loyka argues that in the past decade, poverty and inequality have declined in Latin America. He claims that part of the explanation is the rise of left-leaning governments and a departure from neoliberal reforms. He gives two examples of countries that have reduced poverty and in-equality—Brazil and Chile—noting how social programs were used in both countries to lower poverty rates and reduce in-equality. He concludes that continued progressive spending will be needed in Latin America to continue the progress. Loyka is communications and development assistant at the World Policy Institute.

As you read, consider the following questions:

1. According to the author, what percentage of the popula-tion of Latin America lived in poverty in 2010?

2. What percentage of the population of Brazil lives in a household that receives social security benefits, accord-ing to Loyka?

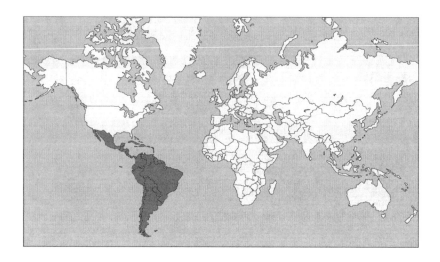

3. According to the author, what percentage of the population of Chile lived in poverty in 2009?

Over the past decade, income inequality and poverty in Latin America have been on the decline. These two key socioeconomic indicators have historically plagued the region, inhibiting it from prospering. Although most of the countries in Latin America and the Caribbean still suffer from very high levels of inequality and poverty, the region has made important initial strides in reducing these statistics. Some countries have improved far more than others, when measured by the Gini index, a statistical measurement for inequality ranging from 0 to 1. For example, Uruguay, at .433 in 2009, and Venezuela, at .412 in 2008, recorded lower Gini coefficients than the United States (.468) in 2009. Peru (.469), El Salvador (.478), Ecuador (.500) and Costa Rica (.501) all recorded Gini coefficients within range of the United States; and in 2009, Argentina, Chile and Uruguay each had lower poverty rates than the United States.

Poverty and Inequality in Latin America

The effects of poverty and inequality can prove devastating on the social and economic landscapes of a country and a region.

Income inequality and economic growth are likely to directly impact poverty, as both high economic growth and a greater degree of equality in income distribution will help to alleviate poverty. It is true that strong economic growth has helped to reduce poverty in Latin America. However, scholars have noted that the reduction of inequality and poverty over the past decade is partially due to increased levels of effective income distribution, in addition to the reduction in the earnings gap between high- and low-skilled workers. Policies that have been introduced to increase and yield such results include increased spending on education as well as conditional cash transfer programs (CCT)—a monthly grant to low-income households attached to requirements such as mandatory school attendance. *Bolsa Família* in Brazil, *Chile Solidario* in Chile and their objectives are examples of such programs.

Although most of the countries in Latin America and the Caribbean still suffer from very high levels of inequality and poverty, the region has made important initial strides in reducing these statistics.

Due to strategic counter-cyclical spending measures, the Latin American economy was able to recover from the 2008 economic crisis faster than other regions. Following a 1.9 percent decline in GDP [gross domestic product] for 2009, the region's economy grew by 6 percent in 2010. Regional poverty levels, which had increased slightly in 2008, bounced back to pre-crisis levels in 2010. In 2008, at the height of the crisis, 33 percent of the region's population lived in poverty. After increasing to 33.1 percent in 2009, this number dropped to 32.1 percent in 2010. Many economists and scholars attribute this slight, yet important, success to the recovery and growth of the economy. The regional economy has been projected to grow 4.7 percent in 2011 and to continue to show positive growth in the years to come; however, this does not mean that the social spending and transfer programs of the past decade should be reduced or terminated in the post-crisis decade. As we have learned from the global economic crisis, as well as from past crises, many external factors can inhibit or even halt economic growth. In order to effectively reduce poverty, income inequality must be reduced. The reduction of inequality, and therefore poverty, most likely will be attained through efficient and substantial social spending and transfer programs.

In the 1990s, Latin America was assaulted by a wave of neoliberal reforms. These reforms were accompanied by an increase in inequality and poverty, which were largely reversed in the following decade. In response, a wave of left-leaning governments took power in Latin America during the 2000s, during which time both inequality and poverty declined. Despite Brazil's and Chile's strikingly contrasting levels of inequality and poverty, these countries have instituted development models based on strategies of effective pro-poor policy making in the 21st century. Brazil has retained its historically high levels of inequality and poverty, whereas Chile has experienced lesser amounts of both. Nonetheless, these two regional economic and political powerhouses have managed to continue their push to reduce poverty and inequality, while encouraging growth and setting forth an optimistic example for the region through beneficial social spending and economic transfer programs.

Brazil's Reduction in Poverty and Inequality

Although Brazil historically has experienced one of the highest levels of inequality and poverty in the world, over the past decade, the region's largest country has made great strides in reducing the magnitude of its numbers. In 2001, Brazil's Gini coefficient on income inequality was .558, an extremely high figure. By 2009, it had reduced that value to .537; still very high, but a solid decrease. Additionally, the percentage of persons living in poverty in 2001 was 37.5 percent, while those living in indigence were 13.2 percent. Fortunately, by 2009, poverty had been reduced to 24.9 percent and its level of indigence to 7 percent. In fact, Brazil met its first Millennium Development Goal by reducing the proportion of the population living in extreme poverty by half, almost a decade before the 2015 deadline. According to the Economic Commission [for] Latin America and the Caribbean, distribution contributed to 54 percent of the decline in poverty from 2001 to 2009, whereas economic growth contributed to 46 percent. Therefore, while Brazil's strong economic growth has played an important role in raising overall wealth in the country, its politically mandated social policies have certainly helped to distribute it.

A wave of left-leaning governments took power in Latin America during the 2000s, during which time both inequality and poverty declined.

Between 2001 and 2007, the per capita income of the poorest 10 percent of the Brazilian population grew by 7 percent per year. The national average in per capita growth was 2.5 percent, but only 1.1 percent for the richest 10 percent of the population. Therefore, the poor's income growth has been far greater than in comparison with the country's rich. Brazil was able to accomplish such a feat through the growth of both its labor income, in which inequality was reduced with the expansion of education, along with non-labor income, in which inequality was reduced through efforts in public transfers and social security; yet, non-labor income decidedly played a greater role. Public transfers accounted for over 80 percent of Brazilian families' non-labor income and for 49 percent of the total reduction in non-labor income inequality.

Brazil's most famous and effective CCT is *Bolsa Família*. This program aims at eliminating both short-term and long-term poverty through immediate cash transfers and long-term investment in the country's human development. *Bolsa Família* is the successor to previous CCTs implemented in 1999 by the [Fernando Henrique] Cardoso administration. In 2003, President Luiz Inácio Lula da Silva of the *Partido dos Trabalhadores* (PT) expanded the program and was able to increase the number of families partaking in the *Bolsa Família* program from 6.5 million in 2004 to 11 million by 2006. Currently, there are more than 12 million family recipients. In June 2011, President Dilma Rousseff announced the "Brazil Without Misery" plan, which aims to eliminate dire poverty by 2014. The plan aspires to improve access to public services, such as education, health care, running water, electricity and sewage; improve vocational training and micro-credit; and extend the coverage of *Bolsa Família*. The CCT program will now benefit an additional 1.3 million children.

In addition, changes in social security benefits contributed to 30 percent of the overall decline in non-labor income inequality. Social security has the largest coverage of all public transfer programs in Brazil, as 30 percent of the population lives in a household that receives social security benefits. Also, reductions in labor income inequality have been linked to the expansion of education. Educational equality in Brazil has been on the rise over the past decade as a result of increased public spending in education, along with greater enrollment numbers. Net secondary school enrollment increased by 13 percent between 2000 and 2008, from 68.5 percent to 81.5 percent. The reduction of education inequality, along with the expansion of enrollment in schools, has been a direct result of the PT's policies.

The expansion of *Bolsa Família*, together with changes in social security and increases in public education spending and enrollment—all initiatives implemented by the PT—have played an important role in reducing inequality and poverty in Brazil. But while Brazil has made significant strides, it still faces a long road ahead. Its role as regional leader will depend not only upon reduction of these two important factors, but also on continued economic growth. If the progressive spending measures taken over the past decade are to be continued, and even enhanced, it may be realistic to anticipate the prospect of greater equality.

Chile's Low Levels of Poverty and Inequality

Compared to Brazil, as well as other Latin American countries, Chile historically has had lower levels of inequality and poverty. Chile experienced significant economic growth in the late 20th and early 21st centuries, earning the moniker of the "Chilean Miracle." There is no denying that the country's economic growth had played a vital role in the reduction of poverty after the brutal military dictatorship of Augusto Pinochet; nevertheless, until 2000, income inequality had been on the rise in Chile. Each *Concertación* [coalition of political parties] president produced different effects on poverty and inequality, as their social spending policies lacked homogeneity. However, after 2000 and the presidency of Ricardo Lagos, income inequality and poverty began to decline in Chile. The percentage of Chileans living in poverty in 2000 was at 20.2 percent, and by 2009, that percentage had fallen to 11.5 percent. By way of comparison, the official poverty rate in the United States in 2009 was 14.3 percent. Indigence levels also fell in those respective years, from 5.6 percent to 3.6 percent.

Educational equality in Brazil has been on the rise over the past decade as a result of increased public spending in education, along with greater enrollment numbers.

In addition to economic growth, social spending (and to some extent cash transfers) has played an important role in the reduction of inequality and poverty. As a result of changes

Inequality and Democracy

Inequality is currently a key issue on the agenda in Latin America, and the evidence suggests that it will continue to be. Latin America is the most inequitable region in the world, presenting lower results than regions with more dramatic poverty levels such as Africa and parts of Asia. . . .

This is the most pressing problem on Latin America's agenda. The countries of the region have found ways to put its democratic institutions back together after decades of authoritarian governments and have managed to insert themselves in world markets, achieve economic growth, and mitigate the plights of individuals living in poverty. But serious social problems persist.

Inequality impacts various political, economic and cultural phenomena. It is mainly expressed in access to several types of power (or lack thereof) and thus contributes to its own reproduction, as those who have power have few incentives to effect change. These issues present a challenge to the stability of both political democracy, which is forced to face demands for increased participation and representation, and to social democracy, given the existence of social groups with disparate opportunities for development, which are reproduced in vicious cycles.

Latin American Center for Rural Development (RIMISP),
"Poverty and Inequality: Latin American Report 2011, Summary,"
March 2012.

in social policy, per capita social spending increased from USD [US dollar] 686 (2000 constant price) in 1998–9 to USD 945 (2000 constant price) in 2008–9. Social spending on education (as a percentage of GDP) also increased during this period, from 3.6 percent in 1998–9 to 4.3 percent in 2008–9.

Education has proven to be an essential factor in lessening inequality between low-skilled and high-skilled labor wages. When Michelle Bachelet assumed the presidency of Chile in 2006, she attempted to make equality and personal protection a main priority of her administration. She aimed to do so by creating a universal minimum state pension, extending free health care for numerous illnesses, and building crèches for poor children. These efforts have put Chile on track to accomplish all eight of the UN's [United Nations'] Millennium Development objectives by 2015, making it the only Latin American and Caribbean country to do so. Chile's current CCT, *Chile Solidario*, was created in 2000 and implemented in 2003 by social democratic president Ricardo Lagos. It replaced the prior CCT program, *Subsidio Unico Familiar,* which had been created in 1990. The conditions of the current program include mandatory school attendance and health checkups for all family members; it also assigns a social worker to each Chilean family. Yet, unlike Brazil's *Bolsa Família, Chile Solidario* targets only the poorest section of the population.

Until 2000, income inequality had been on the rise in Chile.

Chile was one of the few Latin American countries that had practiced an effective counter-cyclical spending policy prior to the global economic crisis. The Bachelet administration had saved money during the boom period through its Economic and Social Stabilization Fund. Prior to the crisis, USD 18.1 billion from copper production had been invested in the sovereign wealth fund, which later helped to finance the economic stimulus implemented during the crisis, including increased benefits for the poor. Chile's strong economic growth, combined with robust social spending and well conceptualized counter-cyclical spending, had contributed to some of the lowest levels of inequality and poverty in Latin America.

As the Chilean economy rebounds, President Sebastián Piñera will need to continue to strengthen social spending policies that were so effectively implemented under the more recent *Concertación* presidents.

A Path Toward Continued Progress

Although considerable progress has been made in reducing inequality and poverty in Latin America, many countries continue to be plagued by a range of detrimental socioeconomic factors and have a lengthy road ahead to travel. Without effective, if not aggressive policy making, there will be little hope in breaking the cycle of inequality and poverty. As regional economies grow, as is projected in the years to come, they should be met with progressive social spending initiatives that have been proven to reduce inequality and poverty over the past decade. The examples of left-leaning, social democratic policies of both the PT in Brazil and the *Concertación* in Chile indicate that their social programs can be effective when carefully crafted and implemented, with some consistent fidelity to principles.

Statistics illustrate that over the past decade, left-leaning governments in Latin America have experienced relatively equitable economic growth compared to the performance levels of right-leaning governments, while reducing inequality and poverty at a greater level. Of course, no single universal policy prescription can be prescribed as an elixir that will function equally well in every Latin American country. Unique factors including size, intrinsic wealth, benign institutions and economic markets will often differentiate one country from another. Yet, progressive spending in Latin America, even in many different forms, has proven to be effective in reducing inequality and poverty.

It will, most likely, be much easier for middle-to-upper income countries, such as Brazil and Chile, to implement these types of ameliorative policies. These countries have the funds to pay for social programs and public transfers such as CCTs, as well as to invest in public education. Smaller, poorer countries encounter more difficulties due to their shortage of government funds and traditionally slower pace of economic growth. One option for the poorer countries is to look toward more mature economic policies that promote regional integration and cooperation, or find niche markets in order to grow their economies. Another option is to seek funding from other regional institutions such as *Banco del Sur* (Bank of the South), which can provide loans with more favorable rates and terms than the IMF [International Monetary Fund] or the World Bank are prepared to promote. Richer countries, such as Brazil, Argentina and Venezuela, can help fund these projects through investment in the regional bank, while increasing regional cooperation. Meanwhile, both low-income and middle-income countries should continue their counter-cyclical spending policies that already have helped them recover from the global economic crisis, as such policies allow a country to save during good times, while spending (e.g., social spending) during the bad.

Left-leaning governments in Latin America have experienced relatively equitable economic growth compared to the performance levels of right-leaning governments.

Some economists and social scientists have predicted that the current decade will be the "Decade of Latin America." Although current projections do not necessarily support such an optimistic viewpoint, they do indicate that Latin America will continue to grow at a steady, moderate pace. In looking back at the progress that has been made in reducing inequality and poverty over the past decade, it is not unreasonable to predict that progress in the hemisphere will continue into the current decade. How it all plays out, however, will depend upon the degree of dedication that this generation of leaders has in choosing policies that reasonably serve their constituents.

In Europe, the Economic Recession Has Increased Inequality

Hanan Morsy

In the following viewpoint, Hanan Morsy argues that the global economic crisis caused increased unemployment in Europe that has exacerbated inequality. Morsy claims that whereas unemployment worsens inequality, social safety nets and job opportunities for vulnerable groups reduce inequality. She concludes that European countries need to take several steps to protect vulnerable groups from unemployment in order to reduce inequality. Morsy is senior regional economist in charge of the Southern Mediterranean at the European Bank for Reconstruction and Development.

As you read, consider the following questions:

1. In which four countries does the author claim that the rise in unemployment during the economic crisis increased inequality by as much as 10 percentage points?

2. According to Morsy, does a two-tier employment system of temporary and permanent workers worsen or reduce inequality?

Hanan Morsy, "Unemployed in Europe," *Finance & Development*, vol. 48, no. 3, September 2011. Copyright © 2011 by the International Monetary Fund. All rights reserved. Reproduced by permission.

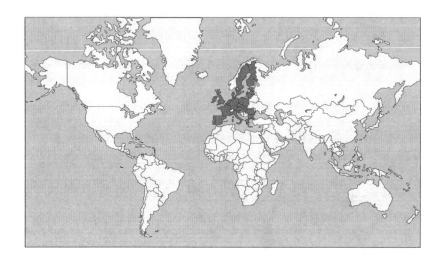

3. The author suggests that European countries attract second-income earners to the labor force by doing what?

The most fragile groups in the European labor market—young, low-skilled, and temporary workers—suffered the most during the global and regional economic crises. And if they remain unemployed for too long, they are likely to lose their skills, become discouraged, and withdraw from the work-force. Unemployment among these groups has aggravated income inequality and runs the risk of shredding Europe's social fabric, threatening its public finances, and inhibiting growth.

To find out how labor market developments after the crisis affected inequality in Europe and what can be done to help, we looked at what caused income inequality in the Organisation for Economic Co-operation and Development countries—for which a strong set of inequality data are available—in the quarter century (1980–2005) before the recent global economic crisis. Extrapolating from the pre-crisis experience, we found that despite the social safety nets Europe is famous for, the crisis exacerbated inequality in the region, mainly by increasing unemployment and inhibiting job creation. Moreover, as the recovery takes hold, how it plays out globally and in Europe itself—which income groups benefit the most—will determine what happens to inequality on the continent. A jobless recovery could further worsen economic disparity and undermine both economic performance and social cohesion.

The Rise in Unemployment in Europe

Overall, the rise in unemployment during the crisis increased inequality by an estimated 2 percentage points in the euro area as a whole, and by as much as 10 percentage points in the periphery countries—Greece, Ireland, Portugal, and Spain—where the labor market situation deteriorated much more sharply. The crisis also led discouraged workers to drop out of the labor force, a factor that is likely to have further exacerbated income disparity. On the other hand, social safety nets are likely to have cushioned the impact of unemployment on inequality.

Overall, the rise in unemployment during the crisis increased inequality by an estimated 2 percentage points in the euro area as a whole.

Inequality went up in most euro area countries as the rise in unemployment rates further widened the gap between rich and poor. Spain and Ireland, in particular, are estimated to have suffered the largest deterioration in income distribution, with income inequality rising by 20 percentage points and 11 percentage points, respectively. This reflects surging job losses as construction-sector activity contracted sharply after housing bubbles burst, leaving many low-skilled workers without jobs. Close to half of the unemployment contribution to inequality in these countries can be attributed to long-term unemployment. By contrast inequality barely moved in Germany and the Netherlands: The unemployment response to declining output was unusually muted because of part-time work programs that supported job retention in anticipation of a rebound.

Within Europe, cross-country differences in income inequality reflect the interplay of labor-market developments, education levels, and social expenditures. In general, the evidence confirmed expectations. Higher unemployment, long-term unemployment, and a two-tier employment system of temporary and permanent workers all *worsen inequality*. And social safety nets, including unemployment benefits and welfare payments; more education; and better job opportunities for vulnerable groups who do not easily find jobs—especially women and youths—*all reduce inequality*.

Steps to Reduce Inequality

European countries can take a number of steps to protect vulnerable groups from unemployment and help reduce income inequality:

- *rebalance employment protection*—with a view to *supporting job creation*—by relaxing protection for regular workers while enhancing it for temporary workers, who are generally the last hired and first fired;

- *avert long-term unemployment*, through *job search assistance, training, and incentives for private sector employment*;

- *improve youth access to the labor market*, by integrating employment services and the education system through outreach programs, training, apprenticeships, and access to job search assistance measures;

- *attract second-income earners to the labor force*, by enhancing child care support and allowing women to file their labor income separately from their husbands in countries with joint family taxation;

- *allow wages to be more aligned with productivity* to provide firms with better incentives to invest and create jobs; and

- *foster competition and a more business-friendly environment* by removing entry barriers and reducing operating restrictions in sectors such as services and retail and network industries.

European countries can take a number of steps to protect vulnerable groups from unemployment and help reduce income inequality.

Only a healthy recovery accompanied by job creation will improve income distribution and strengthen social cohesion and political sustainability of growth. Accelerating jobs recovery through far-reaching labor and product market reforms is essential to prevent the buildup of long-term unemployment, especially for those groups that were hit the hardest.

Periodical and Internet Sources Bibliography

The following articles have been selected to supplement the diverse views presented in this chapter.

David Cooper, Mary Gable, and Algernon Austin	"The Public-Sector Jobs Crisis," *EPI Briefing Paper*, no. 339, May 2, 2012. www.epi.org.
Kemal Dervis	"The Economic Imperatives of the Arab Spring," Project Syndicate, January 12, 2012. www.project-syndicate.org.
Paul Fourier	"Social Model Is Europe's Solution, Not Its Problem," Bloomberg, April 22, 2012. www.bloomberg.com.
John Githongo	"When Wealth Breeds Rage," *New York Times*, July 23, 2011.
Luke Holland	"How Austerity Is Eroding Human Rights," *Al Jazeera*, June 27, 2012. www.aljazeera.com.
Seth Kaplan	"Do World Bank Country Classifications Hurt the Poor?," Policy Innovations, March 12, 2012. www.policyinnovations.org.
Michael Kumhof and Romain Rancière	"Leveraging Inequality," *Finance & Development*, December 2010.
Mutumwa Mawere	"Africa 2012: Confronting the Triple Challenges—Economic Inequality," *NewsDay* (Zimbabwe), July 10, 2012.
Malcolm Payne	"What's So Special About Social Work and Social Justice?," *Guardian Professional* (UK), July 10, 2012.
Sheldon Richman	"The 99% and the 1%: The Economic Means Versus the Political Means," *Freeman*, March 16, 2012.

GLOBAL VIEWPOINTS

CHAPTER 2

Social Justice and Minorities

Indigenous Peoples in Australia Should Be Recognized in the Constitution

Aboriginal and Torres Strait Islander Social Justice Commissioner

In the following viewpoint, the Aboriginal and Torres Strait Islander Social Justice Commissioner argues that there is a need for the Australian government to enact constitutional reform to formally recognize indigenous peoples. The author contends that although symbolic, the effects would have a positive practical impact. The Aboriginal and Torres Strait Islander Social Justice Commissioner, a position currently held by Mick Gooda, works within the Australian Human Rights Commission to ensure social justice for indigenous peoples.

As you read, consider the following questions:

1. In what year did the Australian prime minister deliver the national apology to Australia's indigenous peoples, according to the author?

2. What three principles does the author claim ought to be affirmed to respect the diversity and culture of indigenous peoples as an integral part of the nation?

Aboriginal and Torres Strait Islander Social Justice Commissioner, "Constitutional Reform: Creating a Nation for All of Us," Australian Human Rights Commission, 2011, pp. 2–9. www.hreoc.gov.au. Copyright © Australian Human Rights Commission 2013. Reproduced by permission.

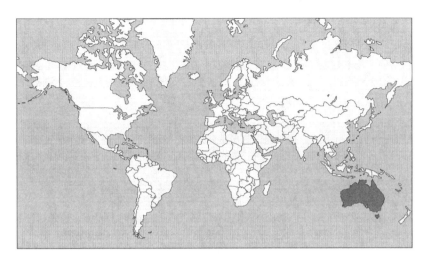

3. What right does the author claim is currently taken for granted by Australians and not protected by the Australian Constitution?

One hundred and ten years ago [1900], Queen Victoria gave Royal Assent to the Australian Constitution, the founding document of our nation and pre-eminent source of law in the country.

Aboriginal and Torres Strait Islander peoples were noticeably absent from its drafting.

We were excluded from the discussions concerning the creation of a new nation to be situated on our ancestral lands and territories.

We were expressly discriminated against in the text of the Constitution, with provisions that prevented us from being counted as among the numbers of the new nation, and which prevented the new Australian government from making laws that were specifically directed towards us.

The Fight for Constitutional Recognition

As a consequence, the Constitution did not—and still does not—make adequate provision for us. It has completely failed to protect our inherent rights as the first peoples of this country.

Former chief justice of the High Court of Australia, Sir Anthony Mason, has referred to this as a 'glaring omission'.

In the face of this history of exclusion, Aboriginal and Torres Strait Islander peoples have consistently and vehemently fought to have our rights recognised and acknowledged by the Australian government and the Australian people.

In 1938, two great Aboriginal warriors stated that:

> You are the New Australians, but we are Old Australians. We have in our arteries the blood of the Original Australians; we have lived in this land for many thousands of years. You came here only recently, and you took our land away from us by force.

These examples illustrate years of advocacy for constitutional recognition.

> Since the days of the [Yirrkala] bark petitions, Aboriginal people have been aware that the protection offered by legislation—ranging from the Aboriginal protection ordinances to the Land Rights Act—is only as secure as the government of the day.... We have long believed that the protection of our rights deserves a higher level of recognition and protection.

It is upon this historical foundation that Australians are increasingly accepting the need to address this non-recognition and exclusion through constitutional reform.

Improvements in the Recognition of Rights

The determination of Aboriginal and Torres Strait Islander leaders to fight to secure our future in this nation has resulted in some improvements in the recognition of our land, cultural and social rights. This has been reflected in advancements such as:

- the fight of Eddie Mabo and others for the native title rights of the Mer people, that led to the High Court decision of *Mabo (No 2)* and the legislative response, the *Native Title Act 1993*, and

- the work of people such as Lowitja O'Donoghue, Les Malezer, Mick Dodson, Megan Davis and Tom Calma in the development of the United Nations Declaration on the Rights of Indigenous Peoples . . . and its subsequent endorsement by the Australian government.

I believe the nation is beginning to come to terms with its true, complete history. This requires the nation to come to terms with a history of exclusion and the violations of the rights of Aboriginal and Torres Strait Islander peoples.

Australians are increasingly accepting the need to address this non-recognition and exclusion through constitutional reform.

A major step in this journey was the 1967 referendum that resulted in a critical change that allowed Aboriginal and Torres Strait Islander people to be counted in the census. It also gave the Australian government the power to make laws for Aboriginal and Torres Strait Islander peoples.

Ten years ago, the Council for Aboriginal Reconciliation identified constitutional reform as unfinished business of the reconciliation agenda, calling for the Commonwealth Parliament to prepare legislation for a referendum.

The most recent high point came in 2008, when the prime minister, delivered the national apology to Australia's indigenous peoples . . . for the forcible removal of Aboriginal and Torres Strait Islander peoples from their lands and their families.

Positive Developments at the State Level

There have been some further recent positive developments with Aboriginal and Torres Strait Islander peoples being formally recognised in several state constitutions:

- The Queensland Constitutional Convention, held in June 1999, recommended that the constitutions of each state should recognise the custodianship of the land by Aboriginal and Torres Strait Islander peoples. Queensland's constitution was formally changed in 2010.

- In 2004, Victoria became the first state to recognise the Aboriginal people of Victoria in their constitution in 2004.

- In 2010, the New South Wales (NSW) Parliament passed legislation to recognise Aboriginal peoples in the NSW constitution.

This recognition provides a good basis on which to build the necessary consensus within the Australian community that Aboriginal and Torres Strait Islander peoples should be acknowledged in the nation's foundational legal instrument.

At the federal level, bipartisan support for amending the Constitution in this regard has been maintained since 2007. Bipartisan support was reaffirmed by both major parties as election commitments in the federal election held in August 2010. . . .

We have reached a critical juncture. Australians have a rare opportunity to stand together as one people, united in recognition of the contribution of Aboriginal and Torres Strait Islander peoples to this land and this nation, in the past, the present and into the future. What is at stake is an inclusive national identity and a path towards a truly reconciled nation.

The Time for Constitutional Reform

History shows that constitutional reform is not easy. As with the 1967 referendum, it will require the open hearts and minds of the majority of Australians in order to succeed.

I believe now is the right time to take up this challenge: for Australia to come together as a nation, as in 1967, to build the consensus and momentum to make this reform a reality.

The Constitution demarcates the powers of each of our three branches of governance—the parliament, the executive and the courts.

The current chief justice of the High Court of Australia, Chief Justice Robert French, has said, 'the Constitution creates the space in which all other domestic laws operate in this country. It defines the extent of [Australia's] legal universe'.

Australians have a rare opportunity to stand together as one people.

I am convinced that building positive relationships based on trust and mutual respect between Aboriginal and Torres Strait Islander peoples and the broader Australian community is critical to overcoming indigenous disadvantage. I believe that constitutional reform is necessary to facilitate the building of these positive relationships.

Equality and Difference

Achieving true equality does not mean that Aboriginal and Torres Strait Islander peoples should be assimilated or integrated into the nation's governance and society. The declaration in its second preambular paragraph affirms:

> that indigenous peoples are equal to all other peoples, while recognizing the right of all peoples to be different, to consider themselves different, and to be respected as such.

Affirming the principles of equality, non-discrimination and the right to be different would celebrate and respect our diversity and our culture as an integral part of the life of the nation.

In July 2010, I voiced my support for constitutional reform to recognise Aboriginal and Torres Strait Islander peoples and our rights. A number of questions were raised in response. Most of these questions went to the impact that constitutional change could have on the lives of Aboriginal and Torres Strait Islander peoples. I believe that there are a number of significant outcomes for us as a result of constitutional reform. I will specifically address:

- the symbolic value of constitutional reform that leads to practical outcomes, and

- the value of constitutional reform in contributing to greater protection of the rights of Aboriginal and Torres Strait Islander peoples.

I will explain each of these below.

Symbolism vs. Practical Action

Over the years, there has been plenty of debate about the value of symbolism versus practical action. I do not believe that these are mutually exclusive, nor do I believe they should be framed as an 'either/or' option. Why can't we do both?

Symbols are an important part of building nations. They are reminders of a collective past and provide guidance towards an aspirational collective future. They are the things upon which practical actions should be built.

The Australian flag, the national anthem, and the green and gold colours of national sporting teams, are all symbols that connect Australians to the nation's identity and inspire feelings about that identity.

Recognition is particularly important for the psyche of Aboriginal and Torres Strait Islander peoples. Academic Waleed Aly recently commented on the positive impact of symbolic recognition of indigenous peoples through the welcome and acknowledgement of country protocols:

> ... I'm frankly astounded to hear lots of non-indigenous people talk about what is and is not tokenistic on an issue

Apology to Australia's Indigenous Peoples

I move:

That today we honour the indigenous peoples of this land, the oldest continuing cultures in human history.

We reflect on their past mistreatment.

We reflect in particular on the mistreatment of those who were Stolen Generations—this blemished chapter in our nation's history.

The time has now come for the nation to turn a new page in Australia's history by righting the wrongs of the past and so moving forward with confidence to the future.

We apologise for the laws and policies of successive parliaments and governments that have inflicted profound grief, suffering and loss on these our fellow Australians.

We apologise especially for the removal of Aboriginal and Torres Strait Islander children from their families, their communities and their country.

For the pain, suffering and hurt of these Stolen Generations, their descendants and for their families left behind, we say sorry.

To the mothers and the fathers, the brothers and the sisters, for the breaking up of families and communities, we say sorry.

And for the indignity and degradation thus inflicted on a proud people and a proud culture, we say sorry.

We the Parliament of Australia respectfully request that this apology be received in the spirit in which it is offered as part of the healing of the nation.

Kevin Rudd, "Apology to Australia's Indigenous Peoples,"
Australian Government, February 13, 2008.

like this, when so much of what happened to the indigenous population has deep symbolic resonance. It's not just that they were deprived materially. It's not just lack of education. It's not just lack of economic opportunity, although those things are extremely important. It is also the denial of the humanity that comes with that and unless you've experienced that ... I think it's extraordinarily difficult to say just how profoundly important that [recognition] can be.... I don't know, I'm a bit disturbed to hear so many people prepared just to dismiss it, when it's not their experience to have.

A senior Aboriginal activist (name not provided for cultural reasons) spoke of the personal impact achieved by the 1967 referendum:

At the time I definitely thought that the [1967] referendum achieved something—personally, it made me lose my inferiority complex.... It made me prouder to proclaim my Aboriginality.

Formal recognition of Aboriginal and Torres Strait Islander peoples within the Australian Constitution would surely strengthen this sentiment as expressed by this senior Aboriginal man.

Symbols are an important part of building nations.

The Effects of Symbolic Recognition

The positive effects of symbolic recognition extend beyond Aboriginal and Torres Strait Islander peoples to all Australians. As noted by Professor Larissa Behrendt:

Symbolic recognition that could alter the way Australians see their history will also affect their views on the kind of society they would like to become. It would alter the symbols and sentiments Australians use to express their identity and ideals. It would change the context in which debates about indigenous issues and rights take place. It would alter the way the relationship between indigenous and non-indigenous Australia is conceptualised. These shifts will begin to permeate them. In this way, the long-term effects of symbolic recognition could be quite substantial.

The power of symbols is that they can inspire action. This in turn can result in positive practical effects that lead to an improved quality of life for Aboriginal and Torres Strait Islander peoples.

The most obvious example of an event that has achieved significant symbolic value is the national apology. On that day, indigenous and non-indigenous Australians sat, held each other and cried together. The nation took a great leap forward towards reconciling with its past. Prior to the national apology, many argued that an apology would be purely symbolic, and that focus should be confined to pursuing 'practical reconciliation'.

Those who argue against symbolic actions miss the fundamental linkage between the symbolic and the practical. Actions that have real and lasting effects on a community are both symbolic and practical.

I strongly believe that reforms to the Constitution to recognise Aboriginal and Torres Strait Islander peoples and our rights will provide significant symbolic value as well as have a profound practical effect.

The power of symbols is that they can inspire action.

This will of course depend on the extent of the reform. How governments and the broader Australian community respond to those reforms will also be critical to realising their full potential.

In summary, symbolic recognition has the potential to:

- address a history of exclusion of Aboriginal and Torres Strait Islander peoples in the life of the nation,

- improve the sense of self-worth and social and emotional well-being of Aboriginal and Torres Strait Islander peoples both as individuals, communities and as part of the national identity,

- change the context in which debates about the challenges faced by Aboriginal and Torres Strait Islander communities take place, and

- improve the relationships between indigenous and non-indigenous Australians.

No Additional Rights

It is occasionally argued that constitutional reform to recognise Aboriginal and Torres Strait Islander peoples will result in more rights for one specific group of people within the nation.

I believe this view is misconceived.

It fails to acknowledge the reality of our existing societies with their own polities and legal systems prior to colonisation. It fails to reflect the subsequent discrimination towards and the denial of the rights of Aboriginal and Torres Strait Islander peoples. It also fails to recognise that the historic non-recognition of our peoples' rights has continuing negative impacts today.

There are parallels between the need for a declaration recognising the rights of indigenous peoples and the need for constitutional reform.

Reform to the Constitution will address this position of entrenched disadvantage and exclusion, rather than affording Aboriginal and Torres Strait Islander peoples' additional rights. Professor Pat Dodson, one of the leaders of reconciliation, has aptly stated that this is a matter of 'justice, not special benefit'.

Recognition of Aboriginal and Torres Strait Islander peoples in the nation's foundational document will redress a history of exclusion, and have the concrete impact of recognising us as Australia's indigenous peoples within the nation's governance.

The Right to Be Free from Discrimination

One of the fundamental rights that most Australians take for granted is the right to live free from discrimination. However, the Constitution currently offers no protection of this right. While recognition of Aboriginal and Torres Strait Islander peoples can be accommodated through inserting a new preamble into the Constitution, change to the body of the Constitution will be required to ensure protection against discrimination.

Aboriginal lawyer and academic Megan Davis observes that:

> In Australia, indigenous interests have been accommodated in the most temporary way, by statute. What the state gives, the state can take away, as has happened with the ATSIC [Aboriginal and Torres Strait Islander Commission], the Racial Discrimination Act and native title.

Relying on the benevolence of parliament to protect the rights and interests of all Australians does not provide adequate protection against discrimination.

Substantive constitutional change is necessary to improve the protection of Aboriginal and Torres Strait Islander peoples' rights against discrimination.

Aboriginal and Torres Strait Islander peoples are particularly vulnerable to this lack of protection. The Racial Discrimination Act 1975 (RDA) has been compromised on three occasions: each time it has involved Aboriginal and Torres Strait Islander issues.

There is no clearer evidence of this discriminatory effect than the Northern Territory Emergency Response (NTER) that affects 73 remote indigenous communities in the Northern Territory.

The NTER in its original application was not subject to the RDA—the federal legislation designed to ensure equality of treatment of all people regardless of their race. The RDA as an act of parliament can be disregarded simply through the passage of further legislation. The Constitution as it currently stands did not prevent the suspension of the RDA. Therefore, it was ineffective in protecting our peoples from the most fundamental of all freedoms, the freedom from discrimination.

In order to address this inadequacy and the historical denial of justice, substantive constitutional change is necessary to improve the protection of Aboriginal and Torres Strait Islander peoples' rights against discrimination.

Japan's Recognition of the Ainu Has Not Resulted in Adequate Social Justice

Mitsuharu Vincent Okada

In the following viewpoint, Mitsuharu Vincent Okada argues that although the Japanese government officially recognized the indigenous Ainu people in 2008, there has been little progress of policies to improve the well-being of the Ainu people. Okada claims that after a century of policies that discriminated against the Ainu, negative effects on socioeconomic status, education, and dignity are still apparent. Okada is a graduate student in the Myron B. Thompson School of Social Work at the University of Hawaii at Manoa.

As you read, consider the following questions:

1. According to the author, what piece of legislation was passed in 1899 for the purpose of protecting the Ainu people in Hokkaido?
2. According to the author, which two articles of the Japanese Constitution are at issue in creating a special policy toward the Ainu?

Mitsuharu Vincent Okada, "The Plight of Ainu, Indigenous People of Japan," *Journal of Indigenous Social Development*, vol. 1, no. 1, January 2012, pp. 1–14. Copyright © 2012 by The Journal of Indigenous Social Development. All rights reserved. Reproduced by permission.

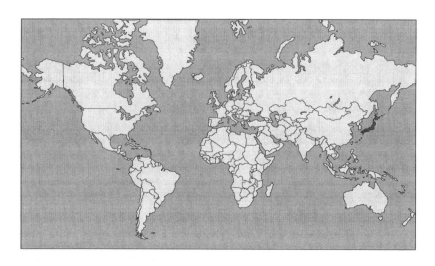

3. What percentage of Ainu people have college degrees, according to Okada?

A major issue in the twenty-first century is the recognition of indigenous rights and the preservation of indigenous peoples' unique cultures around the world. Since the 1980s, a worldwide movement—initiated by the United Nations together with international indigenous peoples' rights and advocacy organizations—has drawn attention to the education, culture and tradition, protection, self-determination and land rights of indigenous peoples. The Ainu in Japan are one such indigenous group.

The Indigenous Ainu People

When the Law for the Promotion of the Ainu Culture and for the Dissemination and Advocacy [for the Traditions of the Ainu and the Ainu Culture] was passed in 1997, the Ainu people were finally freed from the term *kyu-dojin* (former aborigine), which had stigmatized them for more than a century. [Nanako] Iwasa states that the social status and identity of the Ainu people have shifted dramatically over the period since this promotion law took effect.

In June 2008, prior to the G8 [a group of eight leaders from the world's largest economies] summit in Hokkaido, twenty-one indigenous groups from all over the world gathered for the very first Indigenous Peoples Summit. There, they discussed the gaps in policy making, education and environment and economics, and submitted a declaration to the participating nations of the G8 asking to be heard. This summit and many other efforts led to the Japanese government's 2008 recognition of the Ainu as an indigenous people for the first time in history, and the passage of a resolution to create a new law to help them recover their status, regain their culture and rebuild relationships between Ainu and non-Ainu people in Japan.

Much of the literature indicates that issues remain in terms of education, socioeconomic status and quality of life after a century of policies that have enforced assimilation and led to discrimination. The law promised by the government has not been created as of 2011. Exacerbating the situation is the lack of any new policy-making discussion reports or meetings of the *Ainu Seisaku no Arikata ni Kansuru Yushiki-sha Kondan-kai* (an advisory panel) since 2009. . . .

Laws Protecting and Promoting Ainu People

The Hokkaido Former Aborigines Protection Act, passed in 1899 for the purpose of *protecting* people in Hokkaido, including the Ainu people, was modeled on the U.S. legislation known as the Dawes Act for Native Americans in Oklahoma. This act ignored the fact that the Ainu livelihood depended on fishing and hunting. Prior to this act, in the late 1870s and early 1880s, their traditional fishing and hunting activities were banned by the government in order to promote farming and controlled production. The act's main purpose was to allocate land to the Ainu people as a means to promote farming. This act also set a quota so that the land given would be taken away if no success could be proved within fifteen years. Most of the Ainu people, who were not used to farming, did not succeed in their attempts. Those who failed at farming were sent to factories and mines, where they worked as poorly paid laborers.

Much of the literature indicates that issues remain in terms of education, socioeconomic status and quality of life after a century of policies that have enforced assimilation and led to discrimination.

Another purpose of the act was to promote education. Teaching was conducted in the Japanese language. Some Ainu children were forced to move to Tokyo to be educated, but the curriculum was intended to ensure cooperation with the central government. This training enforced assimilation. In the name of protection, the 1899 act deprived the Ainu people of their traditions, culture, land, language and identity. . . .

A law was passed in 1997 as the result of efforts by a team formed two years earlier. The team was comprised of Ainu representatives, the Ainu Association of Hokkaido, the Hokkaido government, the Agency for Cultural Affairs and Ministry of Land, Infrastructure, Transport and Tourism, and by the pressure from overseas human rights and indigenous peoples' groups. The new law declared that Japan would henceforth be a multicultural nation. The Hokkaido former aborigine protection act was thus taken out of effect, and the government's role shifted from *protecting* the Ainu to promoting Ainu culture.

The Ainu Association of Hokkaido characterized the law as follows:

It is an historic move for us and for the nation of Japan. However, this law does not address anything about our land ownership, educational, political, social and economic rights. These need to be discussed, and we need to step forward.

The UN Declaration on the Rights of Indigenous Peoples

Beginning in the 1980s, the United Nations and international indigenous peoples' rights and advocacy organizations have initiated various efforts to promote attention to the world's indigenous peoples. As a result, there has been much discussion of education, culture and tradition, protection, self-determination and land rights. These organizations have served to monitor each nation. Japan has not been given good grades in regard to creating policies for indigenous peoples, but it has definitely applied some necessary pressure (*gaiatsu*— outside pressure) in regard to change.

In 2007, for example, the United Nations Declaration on the Rights of Indigenous Peoples was adopted by the General Assembly. Japan supported this declaration. It is not a legally binding, enforceable law, but it demonstrates the commitment of the membership to set a standard for the treatment of indigenous peoples, eliminate human rights violations against them, and assist them in combating discrimination and marginalization. This led to the Japanese government's 2008 passage of a resolution to create a new law to help the Ainu people recover their status, regain their culture and rebuild the relationship of communities between Ainu people and non-Ainu people in Japan.

The Official Recognition of the Ainu

In June 2008, just before the G8 summit held in Hokkaido, the Japanese government—for the first time in its history—officially recognized the Ainu as an indigenous people, and promised to create a new law and improve policies to support them. The Democratic Party of Japan (DPJ) defeated the long-governing Liberal Democratic Party (LDP) in May 2009, and Yukio Hatoyama, who is from Hokkaido, became the prime minister of Japan. PM Hatoyama joined the *Ainu Seisaku no*

Arikata ni Kansuru Yushiki-sha Kondan-kai . . . as a means to improve the environment for the Ainu people.

Erik Larson and other coauthors assert that the global norm of the movement as an empowered, transnational actor in indigenous rights shapes the potential for the Ainu people to influence domestic government. Laws and policies in the past have affected the Ainu people. Over the last few decades, there have been some achievements: the Law for the Promotion of the Ainu Culture and for the Dissemination and Advocacy [for the Traditions of the Ainu and the Ainu Culture] (1997), the recognition of the Ainu as indigenous people during the Nibutani Dam decision (1993), the progress in the international negotiations on intellectual property meeting, creations of the liaison committee of ministries and agencies (1996), and the Foundation for Research and Promotion of Ainu Culture (FRPAC) (1997), Japan's voting for the Declaration on the Rights of Indigenous Peoples (2007) and the government's recognition of the Ainu (2008).

In June 2008 . . . the Japanese government . . . officially recognized the Ainu as an indigenous people, and promised to create a new law and improve policies to support them.

To influence the government and promote their movement further, some Ainu have chosen to use outsider strategies, or *gaiatsu* (outside pressure), or collaborative efforts with overseas human rights support groups and other indigenous groups from all over the world. . . .

The Japanese Constitution

The chief cabinet secretary requested that the *Ainu Seisaku no Arikata ni Kansuru Yushiki-sha Kondan-kai* (an advisory panel of well-informed experts on Ainu policy) produce a report

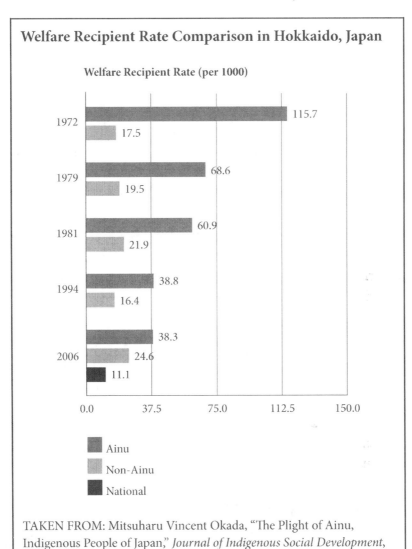

Welfare Recipient Rate Comparison in Hokkaido, Japan

Welfare Recipient Rate (per 1000)

Year	Ainu	Non-Ainu	National
1972	115.7	17.5	
1979	68.6	19.5	
1981	60.9	21.9	
1994	38.8	16.4	
2006	38.3	24.6	11.1

TAKEN FROM: Mitsuharu Vincent Okada, "The Plight of Ainu, Indigenous People of Japan," *Journal of Indigenous Social Development*, vol. 1, no. 1, January 2012.

about its discussions of policy changes. The Constitution of Japan has often been discussed from the perspective of whether the creation of a special policy and the treatment of a specific population under the law would be contrary to article 14, which sets forth the principle of equality. The report justifies the existence of Ainu policy as valid with the historical considerations and article 2-2 of the International Convention on the Elimination of All Forms of Racial Discrimination.

Article 13 of the Constitution has, as its basic principle, respect for individuals. Policies that value Ainu culture and spirituality, including the Ainu language, are important as a means of upholding this principle and allowing the Ainu to choose to live with a strong sense of identity. Addressing gaps in education, socioeconomic status and quality of life are crucial in meeting the intent of the article.

The *Ainu Seisaku no Arikata ni Kansuru Yushiki-sha Kondan-kai*'s report also highlights the importance of ethnic harmony. The concept creates a model by which the members of a modernized multicultural nation can respect one another's individuality, culture and dignity. Thus the government has recognized the Ainu as an indigenous people, and with the new policy changes, all of Japanese society should follow suit with respect and appreciation for diversity.

Even though there have been no additional reports or activities since the last report was issued in 2009, continued discussion and specific implementation plans will be beneficial for Japan as it endeavors to become a true multicultural nation.

The Impact of Discrimination

Much of the literature indicates that issues remain in terms of education, socioeconomic status and quality of life after a century of policies that have enforced assimilation and led to discrimination. Policies of assimilation and/or discrimination, implemented without negotiation or consideration, have made it difficult for the Ainu people to maintain their traditional methods of living, dignity, identity, beliefs, lands, language, culture and education. In addition, the struggles of the Ainu people in Japan are evident in the significant differences in socioeconomic status, as highlighted below:

- 56.3% of Ainu people are employed in either primary (e.g., agriculture, agribusiness, fishing, forestry and mining) or secondary (e.g., manufacturing and factories) industries with lower wages in Hokkaido (24.2% of non-Ainu people are in the same categories);

- Only 17.3% of Ainu people have college degrees, compared to 38.5% for non-Ainu people in Hokkaido (53.7% nationally);

- More Ainu families receive welfare support from the government (38.3%) compared to non-Ainu families in Hokkaido (24.6%) (11.1% nationally).

Many Ainu hide their identity in everyday life, simply to avoid discrimination and the stigma of feeling ignorant or ashamed of their cultural heritage. Even though today there is a relatively higher number of Ainu people who are proud of their heritage and active in cultural events, society should create an environment in which all citizens can feel free to appreciate their roots and identity. In such a society it would not be necessary to disown one's heritage.

Many Ainu hide their identity in everyday life, simply to avoid discrimination and the stigma of feeling ignorant or ashamed of their cultural heritage.

The long-standing assimilative and discriminative policies have brought forth certain consequences. To seek success and escape from racial discrimination in Hokkaido, many Ainu migrated to the Kanto area (greater Tokyo region). The creation of solidarity at the national level among multiple Ainu associations and groups can be an issue. Hokkaido is somewhat more rural, but the Kanto area is a huge urban zone. Thus education, socioeconomic status and quality of life can vary between these regions. The participation in the Ainu-related activities and events and involvement in the Ainu association, and the means to air opinions may also differ between the Ainu people in Hokkaido and Kanto area.

A Lack of Progress

A particular dynamic has been brought into play as a means to change the behavior of Ainu society. The sequence of laws has engendered different characteristics among the different generations of Ainu society. The generation right after the enforcement of assimilation had no other choice if it wanted to survive. They endeavored to act like Japanese, speak Japanese and farm for a living instead of hunting and fishing. They became the hidden generation. They did not teach their children the Ainu language, culture and traditions. However, their struggle, frustration and anger instilled in their children a desire to seek their roots and identity. The children did not speak the Ainu language and were not familiar with Ainu traditions; instead they sought a way to fight to get their rights back. Many members of that succeeding generation spent much time protesting and engaging in other political acts.

The Japanese government has been reluctant to discuss injustices attributable to laws, which oppressed Ainu for the purpose of political gain.

[Naomi] Shimazaki pointed out the difficulty of taking opportunities and developing leadership, particularly among people of the younger generation. Ainu have been invited to leadership programs such as the Advancement of Maori Opportunity (AMO) in Aotearoa (New Zealand) and the Americans for Indian Opportunity (AIO). They attended workshops and leadership seminars as observers. Given the working situation and conditions in Japan, the language barrier and other reasons, few Ainu youth participate in such opportunities abroad. Shimazaki feels that the opportunities for leadership development have been wasted.

The year 2008 was historic for the Ainu, since the Japanese government, for the first time in history, recognized them as an indigenous people of Japan. However, despite the government's promise to create a new law to help the Ainu recover their status, regain their culture and rebuild relationships between Ainu and non-Ainu people in Japan, the corresponding law has not yet been created as of January 2012. The Japanese government has been reluctant to discuss injustices attributable to laws, which oppressed Ainu for the purpose of political gain. This tacit denial of responsibility continues to hamper any forward progress of policies that could begin true restoration of Ainu well-being.

Ethnic and Religious Minorities in Iraq Suffer from Inadequate Security

Chris Chapman

In the following viewpoint, Chris Chapman argues that despite recent improvement in violence levels in Iraq, progress appears to be stalled, with minorities continuing to be targeted. Chapman claims that minorities in Iraq perceive that their security is in jeopardy and do not feel adequately represented within local police forces. Furthermore, Chapman contends that there is some concern about heightened violence with US troop withdrawal from Iraq. Chapman is head of conflict prevention at Minority Rights Group International in the United Kingdom.

As you read, consider the following questions:

1. Which two regions of Iraq are the main focuses of violence, according to Chapman?

2. According to the author, what percentage of Iraqis overall believe that security agencies could guarantee their safety?

3. The author claims that along with mistrust among minorities toward constitutionally recognized security agencies, what contradictory recognition do minorities also hold?

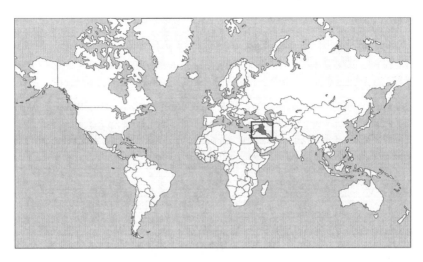

Members of Iraqi religious and ethnic minorities have been targeted by a campaign of violence since 2003, including truck bomb attacks on minority villages in the Nineveh Plains, hostage takings, bombings of religious and political institutions, kidnappings, killings and attacks on minority-owned businesses. In December 2011, this violence spread to the autonomous Kurdistan Region, a normally peaceful area to which many minorities had previously fled in the hope of finding better security. As a result, huge numbers of minorities have fled Iraq; the Sabean Mandaean community, for example, has been reduced to a tenth of its pre-2003 size. Many members of minorities take steps to reduce the risk to their personal safety; for example, hiding religious symbols or wearing a veil when going out, or simply staying at home. Iraq was rated fourth most dangerous country in the world for minorities in MRG's [Minority Rights Group International's] 2012 Peoples Under Threat ranking.

Violence Against Minorities in Iraq

In 2012, Iraq is at a crossroads, particularly with regard to security. The downward trend in levels of violence, since a high point was reached after the bombing of the Al-Askari Shi'a

Mosque in Samarra in 2006, appears to be bottoming out, with 2011 registering similar levels to the previous year. In the disputed areas of the north, which are claimed by both the federal government and the autonomous Kurdistan Region and are home to many minority communities, the withdrawal of the United States (US) army at the end of 2011 has caused anxiety; the US forces played an important role in defusing tensions there. Violence and confrontational rhetoric between ethnic groups have been on the increase in Kirkuk, a city in the disputed areas, where constitutional provisions intended to reverse or provide redress for demographic manipulation dating back to the [former president of Iraq] Saddam Hussein period have still not been implemented. In Baghdad, a political standoff within the government is leading to doubts about its chances of survival in the long term.

Minorities continue to be targeted specifically, even if the reasons for this targeting, and the identity of the perpetrators, are not always clear. According to new research carried out by MRG and its Iraqi partner organization, Iraqi Minorities Council (IMC), ... most members of Iraq's ethnic and religious minorities fear for their safety. In this [viewpoint] we aim to identify the views and concerns of members of minority communities relating to their security. . . .

There are two main focuses of violence, particularly that are affecting minorities—Baghdad, and the disputed areas in the north covering large sections of Nineveh, Kirkuk and Diyala governorates, bordering the Kurdistan Regional Government (KRG) region. The violence in the north takes place against a backdrop of the dispute between the federal government and the KRG over territories bordering the KRG area. Many areas in the north are struggling with a complex legacy of demographic manipulation implemented under Saddam Hussein's regime, which has left communities making competing claims to areas of strategic importance. As was noted in a recent consultation [by the Nineveh Centre for Research and

Development] of minority civil society activists in the Nineveh Plains, minorities are targeted because 'the lack of political consensus between powerful blocs against a background of the intersection of their agendas and interests, meant that minorities were used as fuel and were victims of this conflict of interests, for example, an attempt to confiscate their settlements and make use of them as a political bargaining chip.'

In 2012, Iraq is at a crossroads, particularly with regard to security.

The relative vulnerability of minority communities is exacerbated by the fact that these communities mostly lack militias, but also the informal tribal structures that play a role in regulating disputes that Sunni, Shi'a and Kurds have—structures that were in fact encouraged and strengthened by Saddam Hussein's regime. This can leave them vulnerable to opportunistic targeting, for example, kidnapping for ransom, which is primarily motivated by greed. It should be noted, however, that the hate speech to which minority victims of kidnapping for ransom are subjected, indicates that sectarian prejudice also plays a role in the choice of targets for these acts.

Responsibility for Attacks on Minorities

In many cases, no one claims responsibility for the large-scale attacks on minorities; therefore, debates have raged as to the identity of the perpetrators. In September 2007, the US military killed an al-Qaeda militant, who they claimed was the mastermind behind the truck bombing of Yezidi towns in the previous month. The gunmen who stormed the Our Lady of Salvation Church in Baghdad in October 2010 demanded the release of jailed al-Qaeda militants, and the attack was later claimed by an al-Qaeda linked group, Islamic State in Iraq.

While most of the attacks in the northern disputed areas have not been claimed, inevitably, suspicion is drawn to armed insurgent groups, motivated by a radical interpretation of Islam, who have claimed responsibility for similar attacks. According to this theory, such groups may target minorities for a number of reasons—to create a generalized atmosphere of fear and chaos, scuppering the federal and KRG governments' plans to establish order; to take revenge on minorities, particularly Christians and Yezidis, some of whom have found jobs with the multinational forces (from 2009, the US-led forces in Iraq); and to drive non-Muslim communities out of Iraq. Human Rights Watch found evidence, when interviewing witnesses to a number of killings linked to a dispute over the provincial elections in October 2008 in Mosul, that the assailants spoke Arabic without a Kurdish accent and wore Arab dress. The French Consulate-General in Lebanon reported that it was inundated by asylum claims from Iraqi Christians fleeing Mosul in October 2008, all citing persecution by Arabs. Human Rights Watch further noted that the 'attacks against Turkmen and Shabak villages [in 2009] . . . took place around the same time as a series of attacks against Shi'a sites during the pilgrimage marking the fifteenth night of Shaban, and could thus have been part of a nationwide pattern of anti-Shi'a attacks rather than attacks focused on minorities.'

In many cases, no one claims responsibility for the large-scale attacks on minorities; therefore, debates have raged as to the identity of the perpetrators.

There is credible evidence that KRG security forces use intimidation and commit human rights violations in order to pressure minorities' political representatives to ally with KRG parties in a bid to establish control over the disputed areas of the north. The Nineveh governor, Atheel Al-Nujaifi, stated in a press conference that the attacks on minorities highlighted in a November 2009 Human Rights Watch report took place in areas controlled by KRG security forces, and called on the federal government to deploy troops across Nineveh and remove the KRG forces. A senior official in the KRG's Asayish (intelligence service) strongly denied that KRG officials were putting pressure on minorities in the disputed areas to do anything at all. Iraqi federal government authorities are also accused of exerting pressure on minorities in Nineveh to support their territorial interests.

Perceptions of Security Among Minorities

This tug-of-war between the KRG and federal political block may even be having an impact on how minorities identify themselves. A Shabak academic, quoted in a report of the International Crisis Group, stated that 'the most practical solution is to present ourselves as a separate ethnic group. It affords us greater protection because we live in a dangerous area, caught between Arabs and Kurds, and we don't want to take a position in their fight.' The KRG claims that Shabak are ethnic Kurds, while some Shabak claim a separate ethnic identity—the same being true of the Yezidis. The poor security situation in minority areas also hampers development, particularly where there is a need for foreign investment; even minority communities in the diaspora, who are particularly keen to invest, are discouraged by the security situation.

A further, relatively new development in the security situation is an upsurge in tensions between minorities in the Nineveh Plains in particular; for example, quite serious tensions have developed between Christians and Shabak in Mosul and surrounding areas, over land rights, property development and historical demographic changes.

Most members or minorities surveyed in our research stated that they do not feel safe when leaving home, travelling or at work/school/university, but not significantly more than Sunni or Shi'a Arabs. It is probably unsurprising that the only group to reply mostly positively to the question (67 per cent) was the Kurds, whose region has by far the lowest levels of violence in Iraq. The majority of Shi'a (60 per cent) and Sunni Arabs (72 per cent) respondents answered no to this question, reflecting the fact that all communities are affected by the violence in Iraq. The communities feeling most insecure when leaving the home were Armenians (85 per cent), Yezidis (81 per cent), black Iraqis (79 per cent) and Shabak (76 per cent).

When disaggregated according to location, those living in Baghdad and the disputed areas rate their security as equally low (27 per cent), in federal government–controlled areas (other than Baghdad) the figure is 40 per cent, while in the KRG it is the highest (79 per cent).

Representation of Minorities Within Local Police Forces

Article 9 (a) of the Iraqi Constitution states that:

> 'The Iraqi armed forces and security services will be composed of the components of the Iraqi people with due consideration given to their balance and representation without discrimination or exclusion. They shall be subject to the control of the civilian authority, shall defend Iraq, shall not be used as an instrument to oppress the Iraqi people, shall not interfere in the political affairs, and shall have no role in the transfer of authority.'

According to a report of the Assyria Council of Europe, the proportion of Christians in local police forces in the Nineveh Plains does not reflect their population share. 'Assyrians form the majority of inhabitants in the district of Al-Hamdaniya but constitute only 32 per cent of the total number of police officers. . . . Assyrians make up only 12 per cent of the police officers in the district [of TelKeif] despite constituting at least half of the population.' However, there are indications from local community representatives that this situation is improving, and that the main concern now is over the lack of minorities in leadership positions in the police.

Most members of minorities surveyed in our research stated that they do not feel safe when leaving home, travelling or at work/school/university.

---

56 per cent of the respondents canvassed in IMC's field research indicated that there were representatives of their communities in their local security forces. However, only 27 per cent felt that the numbers were representative of their population size. It is particularly striking to note that 100 per cent of Kawliya (Roma) indicated that there were no Kawliya in their local security bodies. Faili Kurds also indicated very poor representation (85 per cent responding negatively). While 78 per cent of Yezidis had noted that there were Yezidis in the local security bodies, only 16 per cent thought that their numbers reflected the size of their population. Overall, women responded slightly more positively than men, with 29 per cent stating that the numbers of their community in security forces were fair, compared to 25 per cent of men.

The figure for Bahá'i (100 per cent gave no answer when asked if they were represented in local security forces) can be explained by the fact that the Bahá'i religion does not permit the carrying of arms.

When disaggregated by area, Baghdad scored lowest on both counts, with only 8 per cent of respondents feeling that the numbers of their community in security forces were representative. It is of course impossible that all communities be under-represented in the security forces; it should be remembered that the survey registered perceptions rather than facts. The negative figures for Baghdad no doubt reflect the highly polarised security situation there.

Despite the poor figures for community representation in the police and army, there were slightly better figures when respondents were asked if security agencies could guarantee their safety. Forty-nine per cent overall said that they could. There were fairly strong differentiations according to ethnic group, with 92 per cent of Armenians and 76 per cent of Sunni Arabs giving a negative response. Women were again slightly more optimistic (54 per cent giving a positive answer, compared to 47 per cent of men). When broken down by locality, the most striking result was a 93 per cent positive rating for security agencies in the KRG region. An Asayish official interviewed by MRG attributed the region's positive security record to successful infiltration and dismantling of insurgent networks, and a relationship of trust with the general population.

The Impact of the Departure of the US Army

The role of the US forces in Iraq in recent years has been to provide technical support and training to the Iraq army, and to coordinate the combined security mechanism in the disputed areas, a tripartite agreement between the KRG, government of Iraq, and the US, which monitored and facilitated movement of people through checkpoints, and acted as a framework for information sharing between KRG and federal forces. The mission officially ended on 31 December 2011.

Attitudes of members of minority groups to the US forces are mixed. A number of minorities secured jobs with US forces and other agencies, benefiting from a perception that they were less likely to be linked to insurgent groups. On the other hand many see the 2003 military intervention, and the unleashing of sectarian hatred that followed, as the starting point for a dark period in their history, characterized by vicious terrorist attacks on their communities and a mass exodus from the country.

Although these considerations are not necessarily relevant to an assessment of the consequences of the US withdrawal for security, they are likely to colour responses collated by researchers.

Attitudes to the US forces are also likely to be informed by political affiliations to either the KRG or federal government. The dominant parties in the KRG see the US as a crucial friend and ally, whereas the federal government is more ambivalent, being founded on a coalition with a significant number of more or less anti-American voices.

Attitudes of members of minority groups to the US forces are mixed.

Public Opinion About US Withdrawal

With this in mind it is not surprising to see a diverse range of opinions voiced by respondents, with very few unambiguous tendencies. Overall 14 per cent thought the US withdrawal would improve security for their community. Thirty-two per cent thought it would make it worse, and 34 per cent thought it would make no difference. Twenty per cent stated that they did not know. There were again considerable ethnic differences, with 56 per cent of Shabaks saying it would improve security for them, and 62 per cent of Armenians and Yezidis saying it would make it worse.

When disaggregated by locality, the only area to show optimism at the departure of the US forces was Nineveh (31 per cent). Given that a number of observers are predicting tense times in the disputed areas, with the US no longer there to hold feuding parties apart, this is a surprising finding, but one that reflects the above-mentioned complex mix of feelings inspired by the Americans. Diyala, another disputed area, which has seen recent standoffs between KRG and federal forces, was the area where it was most strongly felt that the US pullout would worsen security.

Despite the ambiguous findings, it does seem likely that the US role in coordinating joint patrols and providing a framework for information sharing between federal and KRG forces in the disputed areas will be hard to replace, and could lead to a heightened risk of violence. If that happens, minorities will not necessarily be targeted directly, but are quite likely to be caught in the cross-fire. The combined security mechanism will continue, but with a considerably reduced US presence; it is likely that there will also be an increased role for the United Nations (UN).

As Hasan Özmen, a Turkmen member of Parliament (MP) noted: 'Their invasion was problematic, their departure will probably also be problematic. Some people think the US will leave the field empty so that others can take the opportunity to realize their objectives—for example, the Baathists.'...

The Need to Strengthen Security

From the field research, two seemingly contradictory tendencies could be discerned: a deeply held mistrust towards constitutionally recognized security agencies (and disappointment with their capacity to guarantee security), and on the other hand a recognition that, in order to provide effective security for minorities, there is no alternative to these bodies.

It is clear that many members of minority communities want to see their rights and interests protected—for example, by increasing the representation of minorities in security bodies—but they want this to happen within a strengthened, ideologically neutral, non-sectarian constitutional framework. This appears to fit in with a broader tendency within society as a whole. As Professor [Charles] Tripp notes, 'people support strengthening the federal army and police because of a very poor experience of the last few years with a weakened, decentralized state. They want a state that keeps a lid on local power barons. That is why, in the 2009 local elections, voters took their chance to turf out the militia thugs who had dominated their neighbourhoods, in contradiction to what many observers predicted.'

With the larger, more powerful communities often relying on mono-ethnic or mono-sectarian militias to protect them, minorities fear an encroaching 'every community for themselves' approach, in which they will face the choice of being outnumbered and outgunned, or accepting offers of protection made by other communities, with the terms necessarily dictated by the protector.

It is clear that in the long term, many of these issues will not be resolved unless the deeper underlying political problems are cleared up.

It is understandable then if minority representatives feel that the best hope for securing their rights and security is through strengthened neutral, federal structures, established according to the rule of law. At the same time, if those strong, neutral structures fail to materialize, it may not come as a surprise if minorities' political representatives propose the setting up of ethnic/religious militias.

Some proposed measures would have multiple benefits. Improving the representation of minorities within official security forces, for example, would reduce the economic marginalization of minorities, strengthen trust between community and police, and very likely improve security in minority communities.

Finally, it is clear that in the long term, many of these issues will not be resolved unless the deeper underlying political problems are cleared up—such as Shi'a/Sunni and Arab/Kurd reconciliation, the final status of the disputed areas, and transitional justice issues with regard to Saddam-era demographic changes. However, in the meantime, it is important to take immediate measures to improve security in all communities.

VIEWPOINT 4

Ethnic Minorities in Vietnam Have Not Shared Equally in the Benefits of Growth

Bob Baulch, with Pham Thai Hung and Nguyen Thi Thu Phuong

In the following viewpoint, Bob Baulch, with input from Pham Thai Hung and Nguyen Thi Thu Phuong, argues that there is a gap in expenditures between the majority ethnic group and minority ethnic groups in Vietnam, and that such inequality is growing and needs to be addressed. Baulch is a professor in the School of Business and Economics at Tan Tao University, Ho Chi Minh City, Vietnam. Pham Thai Hung is managing director at Indochina Research and Consulting; Nguyen Thi Thu Phuong is a researcher with the Centre for Analysis and Forecasting at the Vietnamese Academy of Social Sciences.

As you read, consider the following questions:

1. What fraction of the population of Vietnam is made up of ethnic minorities, according to the authors?
2. What five unobservable factors do the authors point to as accounting for about half of the increase in the ethnic expenditure gap?

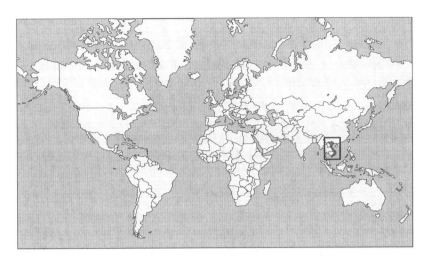

3. The authors identify what four priority areas for new policies and programs that could address inequality in Vietnam?

The rapid economic growth experienced in Vietnam during the 1990s and early 2000s resulted in unprecedented reductions in poverty. The 54 officially recognized ethnic groups within Vietnam's diverse society have not, however, shared equally from the benefits of this growth. Poverty, life expectancy, nutritional status, and other living standard measures remain stubbornly low among Vietnam's ethnic minorities despite numerous policies introduced to assist these groups.

Living Standards Among Ethnic Minorities

Vietnam has 54 officially recognized ethnic groups, of which the Kinh (the Viet or mainstream Vietnamese) account for 87 percent. With the exception of the Hoa (ethnic Chinese) and the Khmer and Cham the remaining 50 ethnic groups mostly reside in remote, mountainous rural areas and are economically and socially disadvantaged across a range of dimensions. The members of ethnic minority groups are estimated to be four-and-a-half times more likely to be poor than the Kinh-Hoa, and are also more likely to be malnourished, illiterate, and suffering from poor health. Despite comprising just over one-eighth of the national population, the minorities accounted for about 40 percent of the poor in 2004. Some government agencies forecast that by 2010, the ethnic minorities will constitute more than half of Vietnam's poor population. . . .

Most previous quantitative analysis of ethnic minority issues in Vietnam has focused on comparing the Kinh and Hoa with the other 52 ethnic minority groups. However, the contrasts between the ethnic minorities are also substantial, so we have developed a seven-way categorisation of ethnic minorities that distinguishes between the (1) Kinh (Viet); (2) Chinese (Hoa); (3) Khmer and Cham; (4) Tày, Thái, Muòng, Nùng; (5) other northern minorities; (6) Central Highlands minorities; and (7) 'others'. This categorisation aims to be functional and is based on discussions with Vietnamese anthropologists and local NGOs [nongovernmental organisations]. It aims to strike a compromise between analysing the ethnic minorities as a whole and analysis of individual minority groups, which is very difficult because of very small numbers belonging to some of these groups.

The members of ethnic minority groups are estimated to be four-and-a-half times more likely to be poor than the Kinh-Hoa.

Analysis of three household living standards surveys conducted by the General Statistics Office in 1993, 1998 and 2004 shows that the Kinh majority has been the primary beneficiaries of the growth *Doi moi* reforms. The living standards of Kinh-headed households have widened sharply relative to the rural average over the period 1993 to 2004. This is true whether one looks at the poorest, richest or average Kinh-headed households.

Meanwhile, the higher expenditures that were enjoyed by the traditionally more prosperous Chinese appear to have disappeared over time. The Khmer and Cham have also experienced a modest improvement in their relative position in recent times, and by 2004 are found to be statistically indistinguishable from the rural average. However, sizeable and persistent inter-ethnic gaps in household welfare are found to remain for the other four categories, with the Central Highlands and other minorities being particularly disadvantaged. These findings are similar whether or not we control for household endowments [resources] (such as the size and composition of families, their education level and land holdings), commune characteristics (whether the commune in which they live has roads, public transport, post offices, daily markets and factories) and the geographic type of commune (whether the commune is located in a coastal, delta, midland or mountainous area). The findings from this analysis also suggest controlling for the type of commune in which households live and access to roads, schools and other public services explains no more than 7% of the variation in expenditures and the impact of these geographic variables has been declining over time.

The Ethnic Expenditure Gap

Between 1993 and 2004, the gap between the Kinh-Hoa and minority expenditures increased by 14.6 percent (VND [Vietnamese dong] 687,000), with most of this rise occurring during the 1998–2004 period. The percentage increase in the ethnic expenditure gap has, however, been more or less constant across the rural expenditure distribution. There is nothing to suggest that the gap is wider (in percentage terms) at the top, middle or bottom of the expenditure distribution.

A number of decomposition exercises were undertaken to explore why the ethnic gap exists. The results, which look at both the average gap between Kinh-Hoa and ethnic minority households and the gap at selected points of the expenditure distribution, show:

- Approximately two-fifths of the mean gap in each year is due to differences in household endowments and community characteristics, with differences between majority and minority households' demographic structure being more important than differences in their education levels and commune characteristics in explaining the gap.

- Differences in landholding patterns decrease the ethnic gap. This is because ethnic minority households tend to have larger total landholdings than Kinh ones, and know how to farm upland and mountainous land more efficiently.

- At least a half of the ethnic expenditure gap is due to differences in returns to household endowments. In academic studies, such differences in returns are usually attributed to 'unequal treatment' of the minorities but they may also be due to unobserved differences in household endowments and community characteristics. For example, if ethnic minority households live further from commune centres than the Kinh, they will benefit less from the construction of roads, schools and markets.

- When the geographical type of commune in which households live and their access to roads, public transport, daily markets, post offices, and other commune characteristics are controlled for, one-third to two-thirds of the ethnic gap may be attributed to commune characteristics. Differences in the returns to commune characteristics are more important than differences in the commune characteristics themselves, which have narrowed over time.

- These findings are broadly consistent whether one looks at the top, middle or bottom of the rural expenditure distribution.

Between 1993 and 2004, the gap between the Kinh-Hoa and minority expenditures increased by 14.6 percent.

The Increase in Inequality over Time

In a separate decomposition exercise we looked at the reasons why the ethnic expenditure gap has been increasing over time, focusing on the median rather than the mean. Our temporal decomposition results show that:

- Around a third of the increase in the median gap between 1993 and 2004 is due to the observable endowments of the Kinh and Hoa, together with the characteristics of the communes in which they live, improving more rapidly than those of the minorities. Household structure and education are again the most important groups of variables explaining the increase in the ethnic gap, with landholdings acting to decrease it.

- Changes in the returns which majority households receive for their endowments and community characteristics, plus the difference between the returns which the majority and minority receive, have contributed relatively little to the increase in the median expenditure gap between these years.

- Changes in unobservable factors account for about half of the increase in the median ethnic gap. Such factors include variables such as culture, distance, language, the quality of schooling and the spatial pattern of settlements that have either been omitted or cannot be observed easily in household surveys.

- Supplementary analysis using additional variables for culture, distance and language that were only collected in some survey years, suggests that membership of the Central Highlands minorities, lack of ability in Vietnamese, and distance to commune and district centres increase the expenditure gap between the majority and minority groups. Membership of the Khmer and Cham minorities and being a Christian diminish it. However, these results are not well determined and vary from year to year.

A major puzzle therefore still remains as to what are the drivers of the disadvantages faced by Vietnam's ethnic minorities. Less than half of the ethnic gap can be attributed to minorities' poorer endowments and their living in remote mountainous areas. Either unobservable factors (such as the quality of education or land) or differences in what the ethnic minorities obtain from endowments relative to the Kinh could explain this pattern of disadvantage. It is likely that these two explanations may reinforce each other, as unobservable differences in endowments may provide a justification for the preferences received by the Kinh. While further quantitative analysis may shed some light on these factors, in-depth qualitative analysis will also be important in uncovering the cultural norms and values that underlie the increasingly disadvantaged position of many ethnic minority groups. . . .

Ethnic Minority Development

Vietnam has a large number of policies and programs specifically designed to assist ethnic minority development. These programs and policies have paid attention to a wide range of socioeconomic issues related to ethnic minority development and are targeted in different ways. Some programs (such as the infrastructure component of Program 135 and 143, the water systems component of Program 134) have focused on the construction of hard infrastructure target in extremely difficult (Region 3) areas. There are also price and transportation subsidies targeted to remote and difficult communes. Other programs and policies (such as the extension component under Program 143, the training component of Program 135, exemptions and reduction for health and fees, and the housing component of Program 134) have provided support for farming techniques, skills, health, knowledge, and housing targeted to poor or ethnic minority households. A third type of programs, typified by the Program to Support Ethnic Minority Households in Especially Difficult Circumstances and some provincial initiatives, targets specific ethnic minority groups, typically those having very low populations and living standards. Over time, as economic growth raises living standards throughout Vietnam, a shift away from location-based targeting, to policies and programs in which the ethnic minorities and other poor groups are specifically targeted is occurring.

The policy process interviews conducted in three provinces as part of this project suggest that these national-level policies are generally well understood and have been systematically implemented at all levels of government. Adjustments based on geography, culture, and level socioeconomic development are, however, made to most policies. In most cases, such adjustments have not resulted in serious dilution of policies, although there is usually a significant shortfall between required and actual expenditures. The most significant differences in local-level implementation of policy that we encountered during our fieldwork occurred in Program 134 and in the exemptions from school fees and contributions granted to ethnic minority pupils by different provinces. Program 134 has its origins in a land reallocation program in the Central Highlands but has subsequently focused on house and water systems construction. The project discovered substantial differences in the way in which different provinces implement Program 134's housing component. Similarly, some provinces have interpreted the exemption from school fees that are given to 11 categories of pupils as providing exemptions for all ethnic minority pupils, while others have not. Most provinces also have their own small programs aimed at promoting agricultural livelihoods among the ethnic minorities.

Vietnam has a large number of policies and programs specifically designed to assist ethnic minority development.

With the possible exception of the price and transportation subsidies paid in poor communes, all these policies and programs focus on improving the endowments of ethnic minority households and the communes in which they live. Very few policies or programs address the lower returns to endowments which our empirical analysis shows the ethnic minorities receive. . . .

The Need to Reduce Inequality

In 1946, Ho Chi Minh famously stated that:

'As people born from the same womb, whether Kinh or Tho, Muong or Man, Gia Rai or Ede, Xedang or Bana, or any other ethnic minority, all of us are the children of Vietnam, all of us are brothers and sisters. We live and die together, share happiness and sorrow together, [and] whether hungry or full, we help each other.'

It is now over thirty years since the reunification of Vietnam and twenty since the *doi moi* economic reforms were first initiated. The process of rapid economic growth has certainly been of central importance in poverty reduction and improving the well-being of the Vietnamese people across a broad range of dimensions. However, on the basis of the empirical analysis conducted by this project, it is clear that not all ethnic groups have benefited from this process to the same extent. The expenditures of the Kinh have risen relative to the rural average, while those of all other groups except the Hoa, Khmer and Cham remain substantially below it. There is also a sizeable ethnic expenditure gap in rural Vietnam, which has been widening in recent years. Some, but not all, of this gap is due to the poorer endowments of the minorities or the characteristics of the commune in which they live. This suggests that measures to improve commune-level infrastructure and the endowments of ethnic minorities as a whole, though important, will be insufficient to close the ethnic gap. Existing policies which target particularly disadvantaged ethnic groups need to be extended. The seven categories of ethnic minority groups developed during this project may be useful here. The widening differential in returns between the Kinh and ethnic minorities suggest some ethnic groups are poorly placed, because of culture, language, geography and market orientation, to take advantage of Vietnam's rapid economic growth. So policies and programs are also needed to enhance the lower returns that many ethnic minority people obtain from their endowments. Priority areas here include:

- Delivering agricultural extension and marketing services appropriate to the diverse agricultures of upland and highland areas

- Improving the quality of education which ethnic minority pupils and students receive

- Increasing the ethnic minorities' access to wage employment

- Improving the Vietnamese language skills among the other northern uplands and Central Highlands minorities.

These and other measures to reduce and dismantle the multiple barriers which restrict certain ethnic minorities from participating fully in the growth process are urgently needed.

By doing this, Ho Chi Minh's vision of equality and mutual interdependence among all Vietnam's ethnic groups will be furthered.

In the United States, Native-Born Blacks and Black Immigrants Suffer from Low Wages

Patrick L. Mason and Algernon Austin

In the following viewpoint, Patrick L. Mason and Algernon Austin argue that despite anecdotes to the contrary, black immigrants face wage penalties similar to US-born blacks. The authors claim that US-born whites have socioeconomic advantages relative to both foreign-born and US-born blacks, suggesting a common source of hardship. Mason is professor of economics and director of African American Studies at Florida State University. Austin is director of the Race, Ethnicity, and the Economy program at the Economic Policy Institute and author of Getting It Wrong: How Black Public Intellectuals Are Failing Black America.

As you read, consider the following questions:

1. According to the authors, in 2008 black immigrants made up what percentage of black America?

2. What is the poverty rate of US-born blacks, according to Mason and Austin?

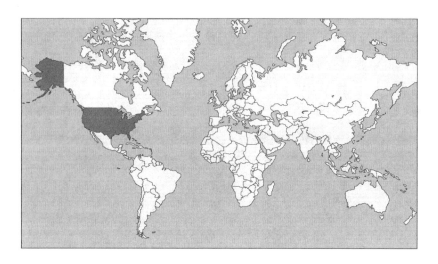

3. According to the authors, African-born men earn how much less than US-born white men?

The popular discussion of black immigrants often exaggerates their achievements and denigrates U.S.-born blacks. One regularly hears asked, "Why do black immigrants do better than native blacks?" In these discussions, black immigrants usually are presented as hardworking, valuing education, entrepreneurial, and family oriented. U.S.-born blacks are often presented as lacking all of these characteristics, and sometimes even described as carrying "victimhood baggage." Many such discussions are driven by anecdotes, and even when these issues are explored using actual data, rarely are comparisons based on more than one measure; rarer still is there a comparison of how black immigrants fare in comparison with native whites.

The Socioeconomic Standing of Black Immigrants

This [viewpoint] aims to deepen the public discussion by conducting a broader, more careful examination of the socioeconomic standing of black immigrants relative to U.S.-born blacks and whites. Its main findings are:

- After taking into account the effect of 15 wage-related characteristics, all black male populations are found to earn less than similar U.S.-born non-Hispanic white men. U.S.-born black men earn 19.1% less. West Indian men, that is, black immigrants from English-speaking Caribbean countries, do slightly worse, earning 20.7% less. Haitian men and African men do substantially worse than U.S.-born black men. Haitian men earn 33.8% less, and African men earn 34.7% less than similar native white men.

- All groups of black women have lower weekly wages than similar U.S.-born non-Hispanic white women, but the size of the wage gaps is smaller for women than it is for men. West Indian women do somewhat better than U.S.-born black women. West Indian women earn 8.3% less than U.S.-born white women. U.S.-born black women earn 10.1% less than U.S.-born white women. African women also earn 10.1% less. Haitian women are the worst off, earning 18.6% less.

- Analyses of unemployment and poverty rates show that U.S.-born and foreign-born black populations are also worse off than U.S.-born whites on these measures.

- Economically, U.S.-born and foreign-born blacks have common problems that need to be addressed.

This [viewpoint] first examines the population growth and geographic distribution of the foreign-born black population, and then compares the U.S.- and foreign-born groups by educational attainment, marriage rates, unemployment rates, and poverty rates.

These comparisons are followed by a more sophisticated analysis of the groups' weekly wages. Multivariate statistical analyses are used to compare the groups while taking into account 15 additional characteristics. These characteristics are all useful in predicting weekly wages and could explain differences in the weekly wages among groups. The reference group for these analyses will be U.S.-born non-Hispanic whites.

U.S.-born blacks typically are found to earn less than U.S.-born whites in these types of analyses.

Economically, U.S.-born and foreign-born blacks have common problems that need to be addressed.

U.S.-Born and Foreign-Born Black Populations

The black immigrant population has grown significantly over recent decades. In 2008, immigrants who identified as black alone or black in combination with some other race totaled 3.2 million and made up 8.1% of black America. The number of foreign-born people who identify as black alone or black in combination increased by approximately 800,000 from 2000 to 2008.

As with the immigrant population generally, the black immigrant population is growing at a faster rate than the U.S.-born black population. From 2000 to 2008, the foreign-born black-alone-or-in-combination population increased 33.1%, but the U.S.-born black-alone-or-in-combination population increased 9.6%. The difference in the growth rates is even larger for the black-alone population.

The black foreign-born population is highly concentrated in a few states. More than one in four (27.4%) black immigrants live in New York State. Nearly one in five (17.8%) live in Florida. More than half (51.2%) of the black foreign-born population reside in just three states—New York, Florida, and New Jersey.

This high concentration of black immigrants in these states means that when individuals interact with blacks in these states they are often interacting with immigrants. While for the nation as a whole 8.1% of blacks are immigrants, in New York State 26.9% of blacks are immigrants. In Florida, 19.3% of blacks are immigrants, and in New Jersey, 15.5%. Within particular cities in these states, the proportion of immigrants is likely even higher.

One does not have to live in a state with a large share of the total black immigrant population to feel the impact of black immigrants. In some states that have relatively few blacks, immigrants nonetheless make up a large share of the small black population. Nearly one in three blacks in Massachusetts are foreign born. In North Dakota, Rhode Island, Maine, Vermont, and Minnesota, approximately one in four blacks are foreign born. Although there are small numbers of blacks in these states, a large share of the blacks are foreign born.

Educational Attainment of Blacks

The analysis below focuses on the U.S.-born, the English-speaking Caribbean or West Indian, Haitian, and African black populations. Black refers inclusively to individuals who only identify as black and to individuals with biracial or multiracial black identities. The black populations will be compared to each other and to U.S.-born non-Hispanic whites. We start by comparing the groups by educational attainment, marriage rates, unemployment rates, and poverty rates.

In the 25-years-and-older population, African immigrants had the highest attainment rate for bachelor's or higher degrees. More than one-third (36.6%) of African immigrants have a bachelor's or higher degree. U.S.-born non-Hispanic whites attained these degrees at 29.5%. About one in five (20.6%) of West Indians have college degrees. U.S.-born blacks and Haitian immigrants have basically equivalent rates of attaining college degrees, 16.4% and 16.1%, respectively.

While African immigrants have the highest rate of bachelor's or higher degrees, they do not have the lowest rate of high school dropouts. Only 9.8% of U.S.-born whites failed to obtain a high school diploma, but the rate is 12.9% for African immigrants. Haitians have the lowest rate of high school graduation, with 26.2% failing to obtain a high school diploma. U.S.-born blacks and West Indians have equivalent rates of dropping out of high school; 19.1% and 19.3%, respectively.

African immigrants obtain college and advanced degrees at greater rates than U.S.-born whites, but they fail to complete high school at higher rates than whites. In educational attainment, the West Indian population is slightly better off than the U.S.-born black population. The Haitian population is slightly worse off. Relative to the U.S.-born white and black populations, the black immigrant population has both positive and negative educational characteristics.

Marriage, Unemployment, and Poverty Rates of Blacks

Married individuals (especially males) tend to have higher earnings than single individuals.

The marriage rates for U.S.-born whites and for African immigrants are very similar. Among those 25 to 44 years old, 58.5% of whites and 56% of Africans are married. A majority of Haitians are also married (51.5%). The rate for West Indians is 48.2%, a little less than half. U.S.-born blacks have the lowest marriage rate at 31.6%.

While U.S.-born blacks stand out with the lowest marriage rates, the West Indian and Haitian populations also lag whites. The West Indian rate is 10.3 percentage points below the white rate. The Haitian rate is 7 percentage points lower.

U.S.-born blacks have the highest unemployment rate. In 2008, their annual unemployment rate based on the American Community Survey was 12.3%. While foreign-born blacks had lower unemployment rates, their rates were all significantly higher than the white rate of 5.3%. The unemployment rates for West Indians and Africans were both 7.9%, or 1.5 times that of the white rate. The rate for Haitians was even higher— 9.4%, or 1.8 times the white rate. While black immigrants have lower unemployment rates than U.S.-born blacks, they still have substantially high unemployment rates.

Relative to the U.S.-born white and black populations, the black immigrant population has both positive and negative educational characteristics.

U.S.-born blacks also have the highest poverty rate, at 24.5%. U.S.-born whites have the lowest poverty rate, at 9.2%. The poverty rates for black immigrants increases from West Indians (11.6%) to Haitians (15.7%) to Africans (18.8%). The African poverty rate is closer to the U.S.-born black rate than the U.S.-born white rate.

When comparing groups by educational attainment, marriage rates, unemployment rates, and poverty rates, a clear pattern of black disadvantage relative to U.S.-born whites begins to emerge. Specifically, on the economic measures of unemployment and poverty rates, all of the black immigrant groups do significantly worse than U.S.-born whites. This point provides some context for understanding the findings from the multivariate wage analysis below.

A Comparison of Wages

When one puts aside the popular stereotypes that black immigrants fare better in the economy, one finds reasons why black immigrants might earn less than similar U.S.-born whites and blacks. As immigrants, they may lack a facility with American

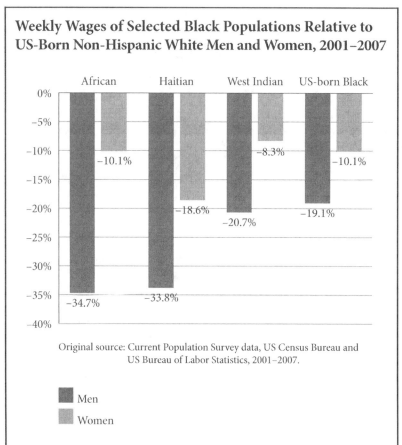

Weekly Wages of Selected Black Populations Relative to US-Born Non-Hispanic White Men and Women, 2001–2007

Original source: Current Population Survey data, US Census Bureau and US Bureau of Labor Statistics, 2001–2007.

Men

Women

TAKEN FROM: Patrick L. Mason and Algernon Austin, "The Low Wages of Black Immigrants: Wage Penalties for US-Born and Foreign-Born Black Workers," EPI Briefing Paper #298, February 28, 2011. www.epi.org.

English and American accents—even if English is their first language. Many black immigrants, especially Africans, are highly educated, but if that education is from outside the United States, it may not be as valued as a U.S. degree. If foreign degrees are devalued in the U.S. labor market, then black immigrants may earn lower wages.

To assess the wages of black immigrants relative to U.S.-born whites and blacks, we use a pooled data set of the March

Current Population Survey from 2001 to 2007. Wage data are inflation-adjusted to 2007 dollars using the Consumer Price Index—All Urban Consumers. We control for, or take into account the effect of, potential work experience, years of education, union status, region, marital status, number of unmarried children, service in the armed forces, unearned income, state employment-to-population ratio, work limitations, and size of locality. In other words, the final results allow us to make "apples-to-apples" wage comparisons among workers of different races and nativity. The analysis is done separately for men and for women, and it is restricted to 16–64-year-olds.

When one puts aside the popular stereotypes that black immigrants fare better in the economy, one finds reasons why black immigrants might earn less than similar U.S.-born whites and blacks.

Contrary to the popular impression, black male immigrants are not better off in weekly wages than U.S.-born black males after controlling for observable demographic characteristics. Some black male immigrant groups are actually worse off than U.S.-born blacks. As expected, U.S.-born black men have weekly wages that are lower than similar U.S.-born non-Hispanic white men. U.S.-born black men earn 19.1% less than similar U.S.-born white men. West Indian men do slightly worse and earn 20.7% less than similar native white men. Haitian men and African men do substantially worse than U.S.-born black men; Haitian men earn 33.8% less, and African men earn 34.7% less than similar native white men.

As with men, all groups of black women have lower weekly wages than similar U.S.-born non-Hispanic white women, but the size of the wage disparity is smaller. West Indian women do somewhat better than U.S.-born black women. West Indian women earn 8.3% less than U.S.-born white women. U.S.-born black women earn 10.1% less than U.S.-born white women. African women also earn 10.1% less. Haitian women are the worst off, earning 18.6% less. While U.S.-born black women are not in the best position among the groups of black women, it would be incorrect to make the blanket claim that black female immigrants do better wage wise than U.S.-born black women.

In regard to weekly wages, overall, U.S.-born non-Hispanic whites earn significantly more than similar blacks regardless of nativity. On this measure, foreign-born blacks do not outperform U.S.-born blacks. Some may be surprised by this finding in light of the higher poverty rates among U.S.-born blacks. But poverty rates are the result of several factors. The higher unemployment rates and lower marriage rates of U.S.-born blacks are likely contributing factors to their higher poverty rates.

In regard to weekly wages, overall, U.S.-born non-Hispanic whites earn significantly more than similar blacks regardless of nativity.

The Hardships Faced by Blacks

When one compares the socioeconomic standing of black immigrants with U.S.-born blacks and whites, the strongest finding is that of the U.S.-born white advantage relative to all black groups. Africans have a high rate of obtaining college degrees, but they also have a relatively high rate of not having a high school degree. U.S.-born whites have the lowest rate of high school dropouts. U.S.-born whites have the highest marriage rates, the lowest unemployment rates, and the lowest poverty rates. Even after taking into account the effect of 14 wage-related characteristics, U.S.-born whites have significantly higher wages than all black groups.

Contrary to the popular stereotype, black immigrants are not consistently better off than U.S.-born blacks. In educational attainment and weekly wages, U.S.-born blacks fall within the range of black immigrant groups. U.S.-born blacks are worse off in marriage rates, unemployment rates, and poverty rates. However, foreign-born blacks cannot be said to be doing well, even if they are not quite as bad off as U.S.-born blacks. Economically, U.S.-born and foreign-born blacks have common problems that need to be addressed.

The fact that black immigrant groups—who are said to be hardworking, valuing education, entrepreneurial, and family oriented—do relatively poorly in finding work, obtaining a good wage, and staying out of poverty suggests that the playing field is not as level as popularly believed. The fact that all of these groups are black may contribute to their hardships in the United States.

In Great Britain, Progress Has Been Made in Tackling Race Inequality

Communities and Local Government

In the following viewpoint, Communities and Local Government in Great Britain argues that progress has been made in promoting racial equality, but efforts are still needed to eliminate all inequalities. The author claims that both legislation and policies have lessened racial inequality, and new policies need to address community cohesion, changing patterns of migration, complex identities, and the importance of class. Communities and Local Government sets policy on issues including community and neighborhood planning, urban regeneration, and race equality.

As you read, consider the following questions:

1. According to the author, what piece of legislation in the 1970s was notable in eliminating racial inequality?

2. What fraction of children in Great Britain is now born into a mixed-race family, according to the author?

3. What two groups does the author identify as becoming unemployed at a disproportionate rate during the economic downturn?

Communities and Local Government, "Introduction and Objectives," *Tackling Race Inequality: A Statement on Race*, London: Crown Copyright, January 2010, pp. 7–12. Contains public sector information licensed under the Open Government Licence v2.0.

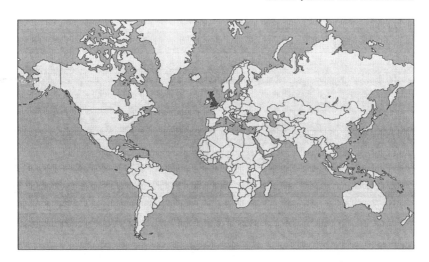

The [British] government has an unshakable commitment to tackling racism and promoting race equality. Until we genuinely live in a society free of prejudice, discrimination, inequality and racism that resolve will not weaken. Our vision is of a fair society where there are no barriers to participation or ambition based on race, colour or ethnicity. Talent and effort should be what decides how well you do. Everyone, regardless of background, must have the capability and freedom to participate economically and in civic life, and to pursue their aspirations. Government has an important role in promoting both, by helping overcome disadvantage and tackling the barriers which hold people back—whether social exclusion, educational underachievement or poor housing—while reinforcing the common values which we all share. Only by giving everyone the opportunity to succeed can we build a better future for everybody in Britain.

Legislative Responses to Racial Discrimination

Since the mid-1960s, successive governments have sought to legislate to outlaw racial discrimination and improve race relations. Most notably, the Race Relations Act 1976 outlawed racial discrimination in employment and services and created the Commission for Racial Equality, which championed equality in Britain for 30 years. Equality laws have helped people access justice when they have been wronged—but those laws have also helped change the way that people think by serving as a constant reminder that discrimination is not fair or justified.

However, in 1999 the Macpherson Inquiry [a public inquiry led by William Macpherson] into Stephen Lawrence's death showed only too clearly the very real discrimination and prejudice that still existed in Britain. Lord Macpherson found that one of our most prized and valued institutions, the organisation which was supposed to guarantee safety and security for all, was failing in its duties. And the charge of 'institutional racism' within the police was acknowledged as a challenge to all public services: within schools and universities; the health service and the civil service. Lord Macpherson identified the fundamental shift that needed to be made in the way government and public services addressed this issue—not just reactively tackling incidents of discrimination once they occur but actively promoting race equality and addressing outcome gaps.

Since the mid-1960s, successive governments have sought to legislate to outlaw racial discrimination and improve race relations.

The major legislative response to Lord Macpherson's report was the Race Relations (Amendment) Act 2000. This was, and is, a far-reaching piece of legislation. It extended the laws against racial discrimination to many aspects of public service for the first time. It also took the law in a new direction by placing positive duties onto over 43,000 public bodies, covering virtually the entire scope of public sector work to:

- promote equality of opportunity;

- eliminate racial discrimination; and

- promote good race relations.

This means that all public bodies must set out how their policies and services will meet the needs of different communities, consider how their policies and services might affect different groups, put in place measures to prevent discriminatory practice, promote equality, and monitor the outcomes of their work. This is a proactive, rather than reactive, approach and has led to a sea change in the way that public services work.

Progress in Racial Equality

Over the past 10 years, a focus on some of the most difficult issues has helped achieve substantial progress across a variety of measures. For example:

- In education, where a few years ago pupils from many groups lagged behind in attainment at GCSE [General Certificate of Secondary Education] level, projects such as the Black Pupils' Achievement Programme and the Aiming High Strategy have helped to significantly raise attainment within these under-achieving groups. The number of black Caribbean pupils getting five good GCSEs has risen by over 20 percentage points since 2003—and the gap which existed between Bangladeshi pupils and the national average has been virtually eliminated.

- In employment, the Ethnic Minority Employment Task Force has focused action to raise ethnic minority employment rates. Projects such as Ethnic Minority Outreach helped thousands of people to get the skills they need to find jobs. The government continues to champion the business case for equality and the benefits of a diverse and representative workforce. The gap in employment rates between minority ethnic groups and the average has narrowed from 19 percentage points in 1996 to 13.8 percentage points today.

- In the criminal justice system, where some of the challenges were most acute, we have seen far-reaching changes. We have set targets for representation, recruitment and progression for minority ethnic officers. We have changed how racist incidents are defined, and made the recording of stop and search more transparent. We have changed the way that police officers are trained, to raise awareness of the issues and ensure they are properly serving minority communities. As a result, the number of police officers from minority ethnic backgrounds has more than doubled to 5,793 in the last 10 years—up from 2,447. We have also seen an increase in the number of people from minority ethnic groups in other areas of the criminal justice system—including the prison service, judiciary and legal profession.

Progress in Equality for All

As well as tackling racism and promoting race equality, we have also made important strides towards promoting equality for all: in strengthening rights for gay people, disabled people, and older people and on the grounds of religion and belief.

For example, we introduced a duty on all public authorities to promote equality for disabled people and introduced protection from discrimination in employment and services on the grounds of sexual orientation, as well as establishing civil partnerships. We have also legislated to improve protection on grounds of religion and belief, outlawing discrimination in employment and when providing services and outlawing incitement to religious hatred—protecting people from hatred and intimidation because of their religion or belief.

We have done all this in the context of our broader work to raise incomes, reduce poverty and tackle inequality which has included introducing the minimum wage and tax credits, supporting the youngest children through Sure Start, overseeing a massive expansion in the number of university places and investing in housing and regeneration.

That has often had the greatest impact on the most disadvantaged families—including minority ethnic families—with improvements on issues like child poverty, overcrowding and the number of families in non-decent homes.

As well as tackling racism and promoting race equality, we have also made important strides towards promoting equality for all.

A Change in Attitudes

Social attitudes and the makeup of our society have also changed. One in 10 children is now born into a mixed-race family. Research indicates that young people are increasingly comfortable with and accepting of diversity—which is unsurprising when this is what they are growing up with, and what they see all around them.

All this is delivering encouraging results. The latest data from the Citizenship Survey tells us that people from minority ethnic communities are becoming more confident that the criminal justice system will treat them fairly and in their ability to succeed and to influence decisions in their neighbourhood.

It's the relentless focus on tackling racism and promoting race equality which has led to those achievements which we can celebrate and which lays the foundation for where we go next.

New Trends Affecting Racism

While there has undoubtedly been tremendous progress over the past 10 years, new trends have also emerged which have changed the context in which we need to tackle racism and mean we need to take a fresh look at the ways in which we promote race equality.

The first is a recognition of the importance of community cohesion. Racism is just one of the factors which undermine community stability. The 2001 riots in Bradford, Burnley and Oldham remind us of that fact. Racism undoubtedly played a role but so did culture, religion, migration, economics and the class structure of those communities. All these factors had helped create communities living separate, parallel lives with little understanding of each other. Data from the British Social Attitudes survey published in January 2010 showed that only a quarter of people felt positively about Islam. The focus on community cohesion has been given even greater priority since the terrorist bombings in London in 2005, with the threat of a minority of people being drawn into violent extremism.

The second trend has been the changing pattern of migration over the past 10 years, including all migrants, whether legal, illegal, asylum seekers or refugees. Legitimate economic migration, while clearly benefiting the UK [United Kingdom] as a whole, has had an impact on the labour market and on wages in some industries and in some communities. In some places we have seen antipathy towards some minority communities become more socially accepted—sometimes aimed at groups such as Eastern Europeans or Muslims, and sometimes against the Asian community more widely—justified on the grounds of religious difference but manifesting itself as racial prejudice. Racism is also achieving a political voice through the British National Party (BNP) and other extreme racist groups. These groups seek to exploit legitimate worries by spreading myths and in some cases, resorting to provocative and violent tactics.

The third trend is that we all have increasingly complex identities. Our race, faith, social class, gender, and any number of other factors come together to create our unique identities. For example, identification with a particular religion strongly shapes many people's identity and how they live their lives. In some places we have seen a rise in attacks on members of particular religious communities.

We must avoid a one-dimensional debate that assumes all minority ethnic people are disadvantaged.

These patterns are sometimes heightened at times of international tension. We have also seen on occasion an inappropriate conflation of a legitimate sense of belonging to a particular faith community with what could equally be perceived as discrimination on grounds of race.

The Importance of Class

The fourth trend is that there has been a renewed recognition of the importance of class. Focusing solely on someone's race or ethnic background to explain their achievements or opportunities is far too simple for three reasons:

- First, socioeconomic status and poverty affect people's chances in life regardless of race or ethnic background. These cannot easily be untangled. Minority ethnic families are twice as likely to be poor and it is often that poverty, rather than simply race, which has a devastating impact on their chances.

- Second, there is a growing black and Asian middle class. Many more members of minority communities than ever before have a degree, a good job and their own home. Chinese and Indian students in particular do much better at school than the average. We must avoid a one-dimensional debate that assumes all minority ethnic people are disadvantaged. Such success stories can be excellent role models for others in their communities.

- Third, for some groups, it is not only class, nor only race, but the interaction between the two—combined with the influence of other factors—which leads to a much more complex and subtle overall picture. We see this most clearly in education where:

   there are greater similarities between black and white children from working-class families than between working-class and middle-class children from the same ethnic group

   children on free school meals—whatever their ethnic background—perform worse on average but poor white and black Caribbean boys fall behind other groups on free school meals over their secondary education

   conversely, middle-class white pupils achieve more highly than black pupils from middle-class backgrounds, despite similar levels of parental involvement.

The Need for an Approach Based on Needs

This rich variety of experience means that there is no 'average' group or person which we can cater for through a general approach. Many people from minority ethnic communities have done well in Britain. However, progress has not been uniform, some groups have been left behind and need extra help. People from different communities may have very specific needs and aspirations. So we must tackle inequalities based on their needs, supported by the latest evidence: Otherwise we will rely on outdated assumptions which may no longer be true and overlook new challenges.

We must also be alert to the challenges posed by the economic downturn. People from minority ethnic communities were disproportionately affected by the previous two recessions, as they were at greater risk of becoming unemployed. The latest data from the Labour Force Survey (LFS) again shows that the number of black and Asian people becoming unemployed is increasing at a faster rate than for white people.

We must tackle inequalities based on [communities' specific] needs, supported by the latest evidence.

Alongside these emerging trends some historic challenges remain, such as the continuing 'ethnic penalties' faced by particular groups in the labour market—in other words a worse outcome which cannot be explained by education levels, age or where a person lives. There are complicated causes for these challenges which vary greatly between individuals but may include direct and indirect discrimination, lower expectations, and a relative lack of social capital—the networks and skills which help people take advantage of opportunities. Of course there can be cumulative impacts. If someone fails to achieve their potential at school it will limit their opportunities throughout their life. Such inequalities and unfairness undermine Britain's strength. Not only can they have devastating consequences for individuals there is also damage to society more widely, with a serious impact on our economic productivity and ability to compete, and on positive community relations.

Periodical and Internet Sources Bibliography

The following articles have been selected to supplement the diverse views presented in this chapter.

Amnesty International	"In Hostile Terrain: Human Rights Violations in Immigration Enforcement in the US Southwest," March 28, 2012. www.amnestyusa.org.
Simon Cotterill	"Ainu Success: The Political and Cultural Achievements of Japan's Indigenous Minority," *Asia-Pacific Journal*, March 21, 2011.
Yacov Ben Efrat	"'Social Justice' Requires an End to Occupation," *Palestine Chronicle*, June 11, 2012. www.palestinechronicle.com.
Equality and Human Rights Commission	"How Fair Is Britain? Equality, Human Rights and Good Relations in 2010," 2011. www.equalityhumanrights.com.
Annie Gasnier	"Brazil Passes Racial Equality Law but Fails to Endorse Affirmative Action," *Guardian Weekly* (UK), June 29, 2010.
Nazila Ghanea and Binesh Hass	"Seeking Justice and an End to Neglect: Iran's Minorities Today," Minority Rights Group International, February 16, 2011. www.minorityrights.org.
Evgeni Klauber	"On South Sudan: Ethnic Minorities and Political Autonomy," *+972*, June 29, 2011. http://972mag.com.
Minority Rights Group International	"State of the World's Minorities and Indigenous Peoples 2012," June 2012. www.minorityrights.org.
Joel Wendland	"Race, Gender and Structural Inequalities in the Great Recession and the Recovery," *Political Affairs*, July 5, 2011. www.politicalaffairs.net.

CHAPTER 3

Social Justice and Gender

In Low- and Middle-Income Countries, Gender Disparities Need to Be Addressed

Ana Revenga and Sudhir Shetty

In the following viewpoint, Ana Revenga and Sudhir Shetty argue that although there has been much progress made with respect to gender equality worldwide, large gender gaps remain in many low- and middle-income countries. The authors claim that gender equality is good for development and offer five policy suggestions for countries to enact to close gender gaps. Revenga is sector director of human development for Europe and Central Asia at the World Bank, and Shetty is sector director of poverty reduction and economic management for East Asia and Pacific at the World Bank.

As you read, consider the following questions:

1. According to the authors, how many girls in developing countries do not attend school?

2. The authors claim that elimination of barriers against women working in certain sectors or occupations could increase output by as much as what percentage?

3. Toward what two areas do the authors suggest that international funding should be directed?

Ana Revenga and Sudhir Shetty, "Empowering Women Is Smart Economics," *Finance & Development*, vol. 49, no. 1, March 2012, pp. 40–43. Copyright © 2012 by International Monetary Fund.

Not long ago women faced tremendous barriers as they sought opportunities that would set them on an equal footing with men. Going back a mere quarter century, inequality between women and men was widely apparent—in university classrooms, in the workplace, and even in homes. Since then, the lives of women and girls around the world have improved dramatically in many respects. In most countries—rich and developing—they are going to school more, living longer, getting better jobs, and acquiring legal rights and protections.

The Existence of Gender Gaps

But large gender gaps remain. Women and girls are more likely to die, relative to men and boys, in many low- and middle-income countries than their counterparts in rich countries. Women earn less and are less economically productive than men almost everywhere across the world. And women have less opportunity to shape their lives and make decisions than do men.

Women and girls are more likely to die, relative to men and boys, in many low- and middle-income countries than their counterparts in rich countries.

According to the World Bank's "World Development Report 2012: Gender Equality and Development," closing these gender gaps matters for development and policy making. Greater gender equality can enhance economic productivity, improve development outcomes for the next generation, and make institutions and policies more representative.

Many gender disparities remain even as countries develop, which calls for sustained and focused public action. Corrective policies will yield substantial development payoffs if they focus on persistent gender inequalities that matter most for welfare. To be effective, these measures must target the root causes of inequality without ignoring the domestic political economy.

Mixed Progress for Gender Equality

Every aspect of gender equality—access to education and health, economic opportunities, and voice within households and society—has experienced a mixed pattern of change over the past quarter century. In some areas, such as education, the gender gap has closed for almost all women; but progress has been slower for those who are poor and face other disadvantages, such as ethnicity. In other areas, the gap has been slow to close—even among well-off women and in countries that have otherwise developed rapidly.

In primary education, the gender gap has closed in almost all countries, and it is shrinking quickly in secondary education. Indeed, in almost one-third of developing countries, girls now outnumber boys in secondary schools. There are more young women than men in universities in two-thirds of the countries for which there are data: Women today represent 51 percent of the world's university students. Yet more than 35 million girls do not attend school in developing countries, compared with 31 million boys, and two-thirds of these girls are members of ethnic minorities.

Since 1980, women have been living longer than men in all parts of the world. But across all developing countries, more women and girls still die at younger ages relative to men and boys, compared with rich countries. As a result of this "excess female mortality," about 3.9 million girls and women under 60 are "missing" each year in developing countries. About two-fifths of them are never born, one-sixth die in early childhood, and more than one-third die during their reproductive years. Female mortality is growing in sub-Saharan Africa, especially for women of childbearing age and in the countries hit hardest by the HIV/AIDS pandemic.

More than half a billion women have joined the world's labor force over the past 30 years, and women now account for more than 40 percent of workers worldwide. One reason for increased workforce participation is an unprecedented reduction in fertility in developing countries as diverse as Bangladesh, Colombia, and the Islamic Republic of Iran, along with improvements in female education. Yet women everywhere tend to earn less than men. The reasons are varied. Women are more likely than men to work as unpaid family laborers or in the informal sector. Women farmers cultivate smaller plots and less profitable crops than male farmers. And women entrepreneurs operate smaller businesses in less lucrative sectors.

As for rights and voice, almost every country in the world has now ratified the Convention on the Elimination of All Forms of Discrimination Against Women. Yet, in many countries, women (especially poor women) have less say than men when it comes to decisions and resources in their households. Women are also much more likely to suffer domestic violence—in developing and rich countries. And in all countries, rich and poor alike, fewer women participate in formal politics, especially at higher levels.

Gender Equality and Development

Gender equality is important in its own right. Development is a process of expanding freedoms equally for all people—male and female. Closing the gap in well-being between males and females is as much a part of development as is reducing income poverty. Greater gender equality also enhances economic efficiency and improves other development outcomes. It does so in three main ways:

- First, with women now representing 40 percent of the global labor force and more than half the world's university students, overall productivity will increase if their skills and talents are used more fully. For example, if women farmers have the same access as men to productive resources such as land and fertilizers, agricultural output in developing countries could increase by as much as 2.5 to 4 percent. Elimination of barriers against women working in certain sectors or occupations could increase output by raising women's participation and labor productivity by as much as 25 percent in some countries through better allocation of their skills and talent.

• Second, greater control over household resources by women, either through their own earnings or cash transfers, can enhance countries' growth prospects by changing spending in ways that benefit children. Evidence from countries as varied as Brazil, China, India, South Africa, and the United Kingdom shows that when women control more household income—either through their own earnings or through cash transfers—children benefit as a result of more spending on food and education.

• Finally, empowering women as economic, political, and social actors can change policy choices and make institutions more representative of a range of voices. In India, giving power to women at the local level led to greater provision of public goods, such as water and sanitation, which mattered more to women.

The Impact of Markets and Institutions

How gender equality evolves as development proceeds can best be understood through the responses of households to the functioning and structure of markets and institutions— both formal (such as laws, regulations, and delivery of government services) and informal (such as gender roles, norms, and social networks).

Markets and institutions help determine the incentives, preferences, and constraints laced by different individuals in a household, as well as their voice and bargaining power. In this way, household decision making, markets, and formal and informal institutions interact to determine gender-related outcomes. This framework also helps show how economic growth (higher incomes) influences gender outcomes by affecting how markets and institutions work and how households make decisions. . . .

Closing the gap in well-being between males and females is as much a part of development as is reducing income poverty.

This framework helps demonstrate why the gender gap in education enrollment has closed so quickly. In this case, income growth (by loosening budget constraints on households and the public treasury), markets (by opening new employment opportunities for women), and formal institutions (by expanding schools and lowering costs) have come together to influence household decisions in favor of educating girls and young women across a range of countries.

The framework also helps explain why poor women still face sizable gender gaps, especially those who experience not only poverty but also other forms of exclusion, such as living in a remote area, being a member of an ethnic minority, or suffering from a disability. In India and Pakistan, for instance, while there is no difference between the number of boys and girls enrolled in education for the richest fifth of the population, there is a gap of almost five years for the poorest fifth. The illiteracy rate among indigenous women in Guatemala is twice that among nonindigenous women and 20 percentage points higher than for indigenous men. Market signals, improved service delivery institutions, and higher incomes, which have generally favored the education of girls and young women, fail to reach these severely disadvantaged populations.

The Need for Domestic Policy Action

To bring about gender equality, policy makers need to focus their actions on five clear priorities: reducing the excess mortality of girls and women; eliminating remaining gender disadvantages in education; increasing women's access to economic opportunity and thus earnings and productivity; giving women an equal voice in households and societies; and limiting the transmission of gender inequality across generations.

To shrink education gaps in countries where they persist, barriers to access because of poverty, ethnicity, or geography must come down.

To reduce the excess mortality of girls and women, it is necessary to focus on the underlying causes at each age. Given girls' higher susceptibility (relative to boys') in infancy and early childhood to waterborne infectious diseases, improving water supply and sanitation, as Vietnam has done, is key to reducing excess female mortality in this age group. Improving health care delivery to expectant mothers, as Sri Lanka did early in its development process and Turkey has done more recently, is critical. In the areas of sub-Saharan Africa most affected by the HIV/AIDS pandemic, broader access to antiretroviral drugs and reducing the incidence of new infections must be the focus. To counter sex-selective abortions that lead to fewer female births, most notably in China and northern India, the societal value of girls must be enhanced, as Korea has done.

To shrink education gaps in countries where they persist, barriers to access because of poverty, ethnicity, or geography must come down. For example, where distance is the key problem (as in rural areas of the Islamic Republic of Afghanistan), more schools in remote areas can reduce the gender gap. When customized solutions are hard to implement or too costly, demand-side interventions, such as cash transfers conditioned on school attendance, can help get girls from poor families to school. Such conditional cash transfers have succeeded in increasing girls' enrollment rates in countries as diverse as Mexico, Turkey, and Pakistan.

To broaden women's access to economic opportunity, thereby reducing male-female disparity in earnings and economic productivity, a combination of policies is called for. Solutions include freeing up women's time so they can work outside the home—for example, through subsidized child care, as in Colombia; improving women's access to credit, as in Bangladesh; and ensuring access to productive resources—especially land—as in Ethiopia, where joint land titles are now granted to wives and husbands. Addressing lack of information about women's productivity in the workplace and eliminating institutional biases against women, for example, by introducing quotas that favor women or job placement programs as in Jordan, will also open up economic opportunity to women.

To diminish gender differences in household and societal voice, policies need to address the combined influence of social norms and beliefs, women's access to economic opportunities, the legal framework, and women's education. Measures that increase women's control over household resources and laws that enhance their ability to accumulate assets, especially by strengthening their property rights, are important. Morocco's recent family law reforms strengthened women's property rights by equalizing husbands' and wives' ownership rights over property acquired during marriage. Ways to give women a greater voice in society include political representation quotas, training of future women leaders, and expanding women's involvement in trade unions and professional associations.

To limit gender inequality over time, reaching adolescents and young adults is key. Decisions made during this stage of life determine skills, health, economic opportunities, and aspirations in adulthood. To ensure that gender gaps do not persist over time, policies must emphasize building human and social capital (as in Malawi with cash transfers given directly to girls to either stay in or return to school); easing the transition from school to work (as with job and life-skills training programs for young women in Uganda); and shifting aspirations (by exposing girls to such role models as women political leaders in India).

While so much remains to be done, in many ways the world has already changed by finally recognizing that gender equality is good for both women and men.

The Role of the International Community

Domestic policy action is crucial, but the international community can complement efforts in each of these priority areas. This will require new or additional action on multiple fronts— some combination of more funding, coordinated efforts to foster innovation and learning, and more effective partnerships. Funding should be directed particularly to the poorest countries' efforts to reduce excess deaths of girls and women (through investment in clean water and sanitation and maternal services) and to reduce persistent education gender gaps. Partnerships must also extend beyond those between governments and development agencies to include the private sector, civil society organizations, and academic institutions in developing and rich countries.

And while so much remains to be done, in many ways the world has already changed by finally recognizing that gender equality is good for both women and men. More and more, we are all realizing that there are many benefits—economic and others—that will result from closing gender gaps. A man from Hanoi, Vietnam, one of thousands of people surveyed for the "World Development Report," observed, "I think women nowadays increasingly enjoy more equality with men. They can do whatever job they like. They are very strong. In some families the wife is the most powerful person. In general, men still dominate, but women's situation has greatly improved. Equal cooperation between husband and wife is happiness. I think happiness is when equality exists between a couple."

In Developed Countries, Gender Inequality Affects Women and Men

Organisation for Economic Co-operation and Development (OECD)

In the following viewpoint, the Organisation for Economic Co-operation and Development (OECD) argues that although much progress has been made in developed countries in tackling gender inequality, gender gaps still exist for both men and women. The OECD contends that some policies meant to help women have resulted in harming men and that even inequality that favors men—such as higher pay—does not always work well for them. The OECD is an international organization helping governments tackle the economic, social, and governance challenges of a globalized economy.

As you read, consider the following questions:

1. The author claims that since 2000, girls have always scored higher on tests in what subject?

2. How much longer on average do women live than men, according to the author?

3. In 2010, how much higher was the male unemployment rate average in OECD countries than the female rate, according to the author?

Organisation for Economic Co-operation and Development (OECD), "Gender (In)Equality," 2012. http://www.oecd.org/fr/general/genderinequality.htm.

The financial and economic crisis has underlined the importance of making the best use of all our resources if we are to achieve sustainable growth that benefits everyone in the years to come—and that includes people. Making the most of the talent pool means ensuring that men and women, boys and girls, have a fair chance to contribute both at home and in the workplace. The OECD's [Organisation for Economic Co-operation and Development's] gender initiative is a measure of the importance of the human element in creating better policies for better lives.

Progress in Gender Equality

But how can you compare the experience of OECD countries such as Norway, where leveling the gender playing field has reached the point of setting quotas for women in the boardroom, and partner countries where women entrepreneurs often cannot access bank loans and the networking that is fundamental to business growth takes place in social settings that are traditionally closed to women?

Where is the common ground between OECD countries where more women complete higher education than men and those partner countries which are still struggling to achieve universal primary education for girls?

Making the most of the talent pool means ensuring that men and women, boys and girls, have a fair chance to contribute both at home and in the workplace.

In fact these extremes are not as far apart as we might think, certainly in terms of time. It is not so long ago—and certainly within the last half century—that women factory workers in many European countries were obliged to quit when they married. Today's older professional women may have seen their mothers refused bank loans without a male guarantor. For many OECD countries, votes for women are a mere 50 years old.

Change does not always come as quickly as some would want, and for governments getting the policy mix right to achieve desired ends is not always easy. But they can learn from the experience of others how to get results, and to ensure that well-intentioned efforts do not create unexpected and unintended new forms of inequality.

Gender Gaps for Men and Women

Years of effort by OECD countries to end disadvantage against girls in the education system have resulted in a situation where girls are more likely to complete secondary education than boys and more women than men graduate from college—and there are now concerns that something needs to be done to help the boys. Since the beginning of the OECD's PISA [Programme for International Student Assessment] tests of school leavers' abilities, in 2000, girls have always scored higher in reading than boys—and by a substantial margin: the equivalent of one full year of formal schooling.

Perhaps more worryingly, the gender gap in reading between boys and girls at the end of their compulsory education has not improved in any country since 2000, and has actually widened in some. This is mirrored in a decline of boys' enjoyment of reading and the amount of leisure time they spend on it. Why are boys less inclined to read for pleasure than girls? Could it have something to do with the fact that in their formative primary school years their teachers are predominantly women and they see reading as a female activity, or are they being given the wrong books? And how to remedy the gap? If policy has been successful in improving female education, is a new focus now needed for the boys?

But that is not to say that there are no more issues concerning girls. Even though more women are graduating, persuading them to study sciences and to take jobs in scientific fields has proved rather more difficult to achieve, of particular concern given a shortage of science graduates in many countries to fill jobs available.

What can be done? More female role models in science, less gender stereotyping at all points, both for boys and girls, would help in the developed world. In the developing world, it is first a question of making it possible financially for girls to continue in secondary education as well as boys by dropping fees, providing uniforms, but also making it safe for girls to travel to school. And also, for those not yet in the situation of the OECD countries, learn from their experience and take care that pro-girl policies do not end up discouraging the boys.

More female role models in science, less gender stereotyping at all points, both for boys and girls, would help in the developed world.

Gender and Retirement

And what about working life and retirement? Well, women come out ahead in the age stakes, living longer than men in all OECD countries, with an average life expectancy of 82.2 years, compared with 76.7 for men. This is obviously a fact that governments can do little to change, but they might want to look more closely at their age-related policies in light of this fact.

Despite their longevity, in many countries women retire earlier than men—the average official retirement age is 61.8 for women and 62.9 for men. This gap is narrowing with pension reforms under way in many countries, but even in 2050 men will be retiring at a couple of months older, at 64.6 years compared with 64.4 for women. And because of the longevity gap, women will still be enjoying four years more of retirement than men at 24.5 years to 20.3.

So are men getting a raw deal? Well, you do have to take into account that since women earn less than men (16% less at the last count), they earn less over their working lives, end up with smaller pensions and are more likely to end up living in poverty. And the higher up the pay scale you go, the wider the gap. In Europe, women hold just 12% of board seats in quoted companies, even though according to some studies corporations with women on their boards and in leadership positions have a higher return on equity—which may help explain Norway's move to legislate greater equality in the boardroom.

And it should also perhaps be noted that women in general are doing a great deal more of the world's unpaid work than men. On average, women devote some two hours a day more than men to extra unpaid work such as housework, child care, parent care. And this is an issue not just for OECD countries—in the developing world, rural women spend far more time than men obtaining water and fuel, caring for children and the sick, and processing food. The same is true for girls, making it more difficult for them to attend school and acquire the skills needed for jobs as adults.

Gender and Employment

Much ink was shed over the fact that at least in the early part of the crisis, more men lost their jobs than women in OECD countries. There are many possible reasons for this—men were more likely to be in sectors such as construction that suffered most at the start, but also perhaps that men were more costly than women to employ. It is certainly true that the unemployment rate average in OECD [countries] in 2010 was 9% for men, compared with 8.4% for women. But it is perhaps worth remembering that during the pre-crisis growth years from 1997–2008, women's unemployment was consistently higher than men's on average in OECD countries.

Tax systems have a lot to answer for too—in some countries, systems are weighted to encourage women to stay at home while their children are below school age, or organized so that the second earner's income bears a higher tax rate when the combined earnings go above a tax threshold. Tax breaks for stay-at-home mothers may not be available for a stay-at-home father.

Gender issues are not going to go away any time soon, for men or women, in the search for better policies and better lives.

"Gender equality must become a lived reality.... Equal rights and opportunity underpin healthy economies and societies," as Michelle Bachelet, executive director of UN [United Nations] Women, puts it. If men and women want to work and enjoy their private lives, the system has to make it easier for both of them. Affordable child care is important, but so is ensuring that fathers, not just mothers, have time off to get used to being a parent and be part of a family—and that they are encouraged to use it without being thought less of by their employers. In less developed countries, it may be about first ensuring that infrastructure such as roads and water are in place so girls have time to go to school and a way to get there, so they have the skills needed for working life as women.

One thing is clear. Gender issues are not going to go away any time soon, for men or women, in the search for better policies and better lives.

Is the Arab Spring Bad for Women? Overthrowing Male Dominance Could Be Harder than Overthrowing a Dictator

Isobel Coleman

In the following viewpoint, Isobel Coleman argues that women in the Arab world are facing a challenging fight for their equality. Coleman claims that women's progress around the region since the Arab Spring varies, citing backward movement in Libya, exclusion from the political process in Egypt, and maintenance of rights in Tunisia. Coleman is a senior fellow; director of the Civil Society, Markets, and Democracy Initiative; and director of the Women and Foreign Policy Program at the Council on Foreign Relations. She is author of Paradise Beneath Her Feet: How Women Are Transforming the Middle East.

As you read, consider the following questions:

1. The author expresses concern about what new policy affecting women in Libya?

2. How many seats in the Parliament of Egypt were guaranteed to women under Hosni Mubarak, according to the author?

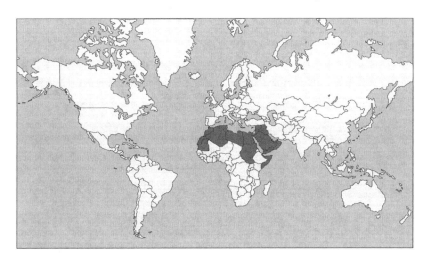

3. According to Coleman, what percentage of the seats in the Parliament of Tunisia are held by women?

In many ways, 2011 has been the Year of the Arab Woman. From the earliest days of upheaval that started in Tunisia last December, women have been on the front lines of protest, leading public demonstrations, blogging passionately, covering the unrest as journalists, launching social media campaigns, smuggling munitions, and caring for the wounded. This month, when Tawakkol Karman became the first Arab woman to accept the Nobel Peace Prize, she gave an enthusiastic shout-out to her many Arab sisters who have struggled "to win their rights in a society dominated by the supremacy of men."

Across the region, though, Arab women are grumbling that overthrowing dictators is proving easier than overturning the pervasive supremacy of men. Gamila Ismail, a prominent Egyptian activist and politician, summed it up when she quit Egypt's parliamentary race in disgust after learning that she would be put third on the list in her district—not a winning position. "We women had a very important role before, during, and after the revolution, and it does not work for us to-day, to accept this," she complained in a television interview. (She ran and narrowly lost as an independent candidate.) In

Tunisia, disgruntled women activists have formed the October 24 Front to defend women's rights in the aftermath of the Islamists' electoral victory there. "We want a constitution that respects women's rights and doesn't roll back the advances we've made," said one Tunisian protester.

Arab women are embattled on multiple fronts. First and foremost are the deep-seated patriarchal customs that constrain women. Patriarchy is certainly not unique to Arab lands, but it runs deep. It doesn't help that for decades, the women's rights agenda was closely associated with the now-discredited authoritarian regimes: Egypt's Suzanne Mubarak ran a state-affiliated women's NGO; Leila Ben Ali, Tunisia's much-hated hairdresser-cum-first lady, was president of the Arab Women Organization, an intergovernmental body sponsored by the Arab League; and both Syria's Asma al-Assad and Jordan's Queen Rania have been active on women's issues. The rise of politically empowered Islamist parties that contest existing laws for women on religious grounds also pose serious complications for women. Although women's activism has clearly been important to the Arab revolts, there is no guarantee that women's rights activists will be able to turn their engagement into longer term economic, social, and political gains. In fact, in some countries, there is reason for concern that women will see their rights erode.

Arab women are grumbling that overthrowing dictators is proving easier than overturning the pervasive supremacy of men.

Libya is a case in point. At the ceremony marking Libya's official liberation in October, one of the first announcements from Mustafa Abdul Jalil, leader of Libya's National Transitional Council, was that any laws that contradicted sharia would be annulled. He specifically mentioned that, going forward, polygamy would be legal, drawing cheers and celebra-

The Gender Gap in Arab Countries

Not a single Arab country ranks in the top 100 in the World Economic Forum's *The Global Gender Gap Report*, putting the region as a whole solidly at the planet's rock bottom. Poor or rich, we all hate our women. Neighbors Saudi Arabia and Yemen, for instance, might be eons apart when it comes to GDP [gross domestic product], but only four places separate them on the index, with the kingdom at 131 and Yemen coming in at 135 out of 135 countries. Morocco, often touted for its "progressive" family law (a 2005 report by Western "experts" called it "an example for Muslim countries aiming to integrate into modern society"), ranks 129; according to Morocco's Ministry of Justice, 41,098 girls under age 18 were married there in 2010.

Mona Eltahawy, *"Why Do They Hate Us?
The Real War on Women Is in the Middle East,"*
Foreign Policy, *May/June 2012.*

tory gunfire from the mostly male crowd. Libyan women expressed surprise and disappointment and wondered why, with all of Libya's pressing issues, reinstating polygamy should be on the front burner. (NATO leaders wondered the same.) Although polygamy was technically legal under Qaddafi, it was discouraged and today is not practiced widely in Libya, but that could change. Female university students, who largely describe themselves as pious, vow to fight this regression.

In Egypt, a number of developments over the past year underscore women's rights as a flash point in society. The inspirational images of gender solidarity in Tahrir Square in the early days of the revolution quickly gave way to ugly episodes of targeted harassment. A hastily planned demonstration on March 8, International Women's Day, attracted a few hundred women but was marred by angry men shoving the protesters and yelling at them to go home, saying their demands for rights are against Islam. Around the same time, the Egyptian military rounded up scores of women demonstrators and, in a show of raw intimidation, subjected many of them to "virginity tests." On the political level, women have been excluded from major decision-making bodies since the fall of Hosni Mubarak's regime, and it appears that few, if any, will win seats in the ongoing parliamentary elections. Their low success rate was not helped by the military's decision to eliminate a Mubarak-era quota ensuring women 64 seats. This was a setback for women's political participation, even though the quota enjoyed little credibility because it had been used to reward Mubarak loyalists.

The strong showing of Islamist parties in the first round of Egypt's parliamentary elections has women's groups worried. The ultraconservative Salafi groups, which took a surprising 20 percent of the vote, openly question a modern role for women in society. One Salafi leader refused to appear on a political talk show on television until the female host put on a head scarf. Another denounced the military government's requirement to include women on electoral lists as "evil," though Emad Abdel-Ghaffour, head of al-Nour, the leading Salafi party, stated that the party does accept women candidates. Yet the Salafi women who did run demurred from showing their pictures on campaign materials, instead replacing their faces with pictures of flowers; moreover, the party deliberately clustered them at the bottom of its lists, making them unlikely to win seats. One Salafi sheikh recently issued an opinion that women should not wear high-heeled shoes in public. Along with Salafi statements of intent to ban alcohol and limit beach tourism, these swipes at women unnerve liberals.

Yet liberals have not been stalwarts of women's rights in Egypt either. The 2000 decision to grant women the right to no-fault divorce (prior to this, they had to jump over the onerous legal hurdle of proving abuse or abandonment) was denounced not only by Islamist groups but by secular ones too—for undermining the family. Other changes to the personal-status laws in the past decade that have benefited women, particularly an expansion of custody rights, are coming under increasing attack. Critics discredit the reforms by derisively calling them "Suzanne's Laws," after Suzanne Mubarak. They claim the laws were intended to accommodate the wealthy friends of the former first lady, and they blame those statutes for a rise in the country's divorce rate. Given the criticism of these laws from all sides of the political spectrum, it is likely that they will be amended by the new parliament, and not to women's benefit.

In Egypt, a number of developments over the past year underscore women's rights as a flash point in society.

Women seem to be faring better in Tunisia. Liberals and secularists have been deeply wary of the rise of al-Nahda, the country's leading Islamist party, warning that it could mean a reversal of women's rights. Since the 1950s, Tunisian women have enjoyed the most expansive legal rights in the region, including relatively progressive marriage and divorce laws and access to birth control and abortion. Since returning to Tunisia in the beginning of this year, Rached Ghannouchi, al-Nahda's leader, has strived to convince Tunisians that his party will not seek to change the country's personal-status laws. Some, however, have accused al-Nahda of obfuscating its real intentions behind moderate rhetoric—a charge that did not prevent the party from surging to victory with 41 percent of the vote in October's election. Thanks to electoral rules requiring favorable placement of women on party lists, women gained 23 percent of the seats in parliament, a higher share than in the U.S. Congress. Most of the women are from al-Nahda and will likely reflect their party's traditional views on women, but their participation in such large numbers at least normalizes an active political role for women. Moreover, Ghannouchi and other al-Nahda leaders so far have been purposefully focused on efforts to jump-start the economy, produce jobs, and reassure foreign investors. Al-Nahda has forged a coalition with liberal parties, and to maintain that coalition, it will have to continue to focus on the economy and human rights rather than getting bogged down in divisive culture wars.

Since the 1950s, Tunisian women have enjoyed the most expansive legal rights in the region.

Ghannouchi seems to understand that while rolling back gains for women can score points among Islamic conservatives, ultimately al-Nahda will win or lose on economic grounds, and women are important economic actors. With high rates of literacy and relatively low fertility, women constitute nearly a third of Tunisia's workforce. Economic reality simply demands a pragmatic approach toward women. Let's hope that Ghannouchi can get that message through to his Islamist brothers across the region. Otherwise, Arab women might soon be channeling their Iranian sisters, who have complained that Iran's Islamic revolution has brought them little but poverty and polygamy.

Women Are the Rising Stars in the New China

Patti Waldmeir

In the following viewpoint, Patti Waldmeir claims that gender equality is widespread in China, engrained in the culture during the Communist era of the twentieth century. Waldmeir claims that the cultural tradition of expecting women to work outside the home, along with an established system of child care, has allowed women to become very successful and wealthy. Nonetheless, Waldmeir contends that there is still a preference for boys over girls in rural areas. Waldmeir is the Shanghai correspondent for the Financial Times, *a British international daily newspaper.*

As you read, consider the following questions:

1. How many of the twenty global female billionaires are Chinese, according to Waldmeir?
2. The author cites a study finding what percentage of women in China aspire to top jobs?
3. According to the author, why are sons often preferred over daughters in rural areas of China?

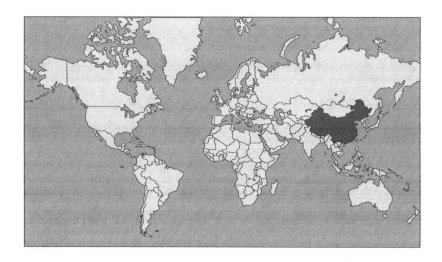

Less than a century ago, many Chinese women had their feet broken and bound so tightly they could scarcely walk. Now the world's three richest self-made women are from China, and 11 out of 20 global female billionaires are Chinese.

In many ways, they have communism to thank. Mao Zedong set out to make China a global model of gender equality, and although he failed at so much else, he largely succeeded in transforming Chinese society into a world where women think they are at least equal to men—and many men seem to agree.

"Mao said, 'Women hold up half the sky,'" says Rupert Hoogewerf, founder of the China Rich List, which earlier this week [October 13, 2010] published a ranking of the world's wealthiest self-made women. He placed Cheung Yan (Zhang Yin), the Chinese head of Nine Dragons Paper, a recycled-paper company, at number one with a personal fortune of $5.6bn.

"The single most positive legacy [of communism in China] was the emancipation of women," write Nicholas D. Kristof and Sheryl WuDunn in their book *Half the Sky: Turning Oppression into Opportunity for Women Worldwide*. "A century ago, China was arguably the worst place in the world to be born female," they write. But as Mr Hoogewerf says, "then Mao unbound their feet".

> *Mao Zedong ... largely succeeded in transforming Chinese society into a world where women think they are at least equal to men—and many men seem to agree.*

He identifies complex political, social, cultural and economic reasons that made a scrap-paper entrepreneur from China richer than Oprah Winfrey or the doyennes of Zara, Gap, Benetton and eBay. But much of it has to do with children—or the lack of them—and Chinese women's profoundly different attitude to child care.

"In the West and Japan, after marriage women stay at home to look after the kids, but in modern China it's not like that," says Wang Jiafen, head of the Shanghai women entrepreneurs' association.

"Women will not stay at home to look after children. Chinese women do not want to stop their career just to be a housewife," she says.

Ms Wang, 60, is now a jet-setting venture capitalist, having retired from a job heading one of China's biggest state-owned dairies. "In China, most women think it's boring to stay at home: they don't have anything to do," she says.

Many Western women might privately agree with Ms Wang, but few would pronounce it so publicly. But in China "there is no social stigma" to such attitudes, says Nandani Lynton of the China Europe International Business School in Shanghai, who has spent 17 years in China.

"Mao made an incredible difference when he said women hold up half the sky, since then it has been assumed that all women in China will work," she says. Easy availability of child care helps: There is a tradition of grandparents caring for grandchildren, and Beijing's one-child policy has meant grandparents look after every child—an impossible dream for working women in the West.

Yin Xinyu, vice-president at Shanghai Rural Commercial Bank, has three nannies, help from her parents and a tutor for her daughter in primary school. "So I don't need to stay at home," she says.

But Prof Lynton says the availability of child care—whether grandparents or child care centres popularised under communism—is only half of it. "It's also very much an issue of what is acceptable," she says. "Chinese women have no role model for guilt, because even before the revolution, everyone who could afford it had an *ayi* [nanny or maid]". Traditional Chinese culture does not stress the importance of early childhood development, so many Chinese women do not feel guilty missing their children's formative years, she adds.

Ms Yin, the banker, says women these days can choose between staying at home or working. "For the older generation, staying at home meant failure, but for my generation, staying at home is a personal choice," she says. "Many of my friends stay at home and I envy them."

But when women choose the workplace, they often prove highly ambitious. According to a recent study from the Center for Work-Life Policy in New York, 76 per cent of women in China aspire to top jobs, compared with only 52 per cent in the US. Working mothers in China "are able to aim high, in part, because they have more shoulders to lean on than their American and European peers when it comes to child care," the centre notes. With an average workweek of 71 hours, the country's mothers would not cope without abundant cheap child care.

Two other factors contribute to the astonishing success of female entrepreneurs in China, says Mr Hoogewerf: One is the Cultural Revolution (think Mao's "Iron Girls" in their androgynous outfits), and the other is economic.

Ms Wang says China's rising economy has lifted all boats, but those with females at the helm have fared better. "A thousand years ago, only men could compete with each other, but in the economic war, you need intelligence instead of just physical strength. China's strong economic growth has created more opportunities for women."

Ms Yin has an even more intriguing explanation for the success of girls: Schoolteachers in China reward compliant children, and girls make more obedient students. "Girls are always being praised in school, and they gain confidence that way," she says, noting "confidence is very important for an entrepreneur".

In spite of these factors, China has not yet found the formula for perfect gender equality. In many rural areas, boys are still preferred to girls, leading to high levels of illegal (but still common) gender-selective abortion. In traditional Chinese society, sons are obliged to care for elderly parents, and their wives are expected to care for in-laws—not birth parents. In a society with a minimal social safety net for the elderly, this has led to a strong preference for sons in more traditional areas.

Gender equality is a legacy of communism that appears to be here to stay.

But urbanisation has significantly eroded that trend too, with many urban families saying they prefer girls because they remain to care for the elderly that males may shirk—and increasingly because they are cheaper to raise than boys, who are expected to provide a home upon marriage, a crippling burden given high property prices.

Echoing a common complaint of women all over the world, Ms Yin says equality in the workplace comes only after women have proved they are not just equal to men, but better.

"Women need to be twice as good to get the same job," she says, although she stresses her career has not suffered due to gender discrimination.

Will the world's rich lists still be dominated by the Chinese in a decade or two? Ironically, wealth may lead to fewer women in the workplace: Women who do not need to work may choose to stay home and, according to Prof Lynton, rich Chinese men increasingly want trophy wives who do not work. But foot binding is not coming back any time soon: Gender equality is a legacy of communism that appears to be here to stay.

In Mexico, Widespread Gender-Based Violence Is a Barrier to Women's Equality

Amnesty International

In the following viewpoint, Amnesty International argues that the number of killings of women characterized by misogynistic violence has been rising in Mexico. In particular, the author contends that there is a disturbing increase of gender-based killings in Ciudad Juárez, in the Mexican state of Chihuahua. The author claims that the government is not responding adequately to the killings, allowing the violence to continue with impunity. Amnesty International is a nongovernmental organization that works to protect human rights around the world.

As you read, consider the following questions:

1. According to the author, how many women have been murdered in Mexico between 1985 and 2009?

2. The authorities in Chihuahua state have recognized how many cases of unsolved disappearances of women since 1993, according to Amnesty International?

3. What court in 2009 found the Mexican state responsible for a series of treaty violations?

Amnesty International, "2. Violence Against Women," *Mexico: Briefing to the UN Committee on the Elimination of Discrimination Against Women*, July 2012, pp. 5–9. Copyright © 2012 by Amnesty International. All rights reserved. Reproduced by permission.

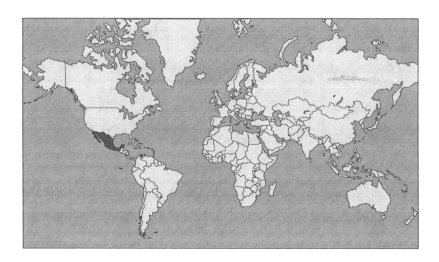

In the last decade and more the Mexican authorities have taken a number of important legislative and institutional steps to incorporate into domestic law the obligation to comply with international human rights treaties, to outlaw discrimination and to establish the right to equality of women backed by national programmes and women's institutes at federal and state levels. It has also passed legislation at federal and state levels on women's access to a life free from violence and there have been gradual modifications to some states' criminal codes. In 2009 the National Commission for the Prevention and Eradication of Violence against Women was established and has promoted reforms at the state level. Several states have introduced the crime of feminicide into their criminal codes.

Despite these legislative and institutional advances, gender-based violence continues to be widespread, with official figures of killings of women rising rapidly in the last three years. The failure of federal and state authorities to ensure the effective implementation of many aspects of the new legislation has allowed impunity to persist. The lack of rigorous evaluation of implementation and impact of the law raises concern about the commitment of many authorities to ensure its success. In 2008 Amnesty International issued a report, "Mexico: Women's Struggle for Justice and Safety," to highlight the ongoing failure to deliver real improvements in justice and protection for women. Despite findings and recommendations of this committee and judgments of the Inter-American Court of Human Rights that Mexico has breached its treaty obligations, the data below on killings and sexual violence indicate the situation continues to be equally grave and in recent years appears to have worsened.

Murders of Women in Mexico

In November 2011, a joint report ... analysed available national data on killings of women and concluded that at least 34,000 women had been murdered in Mexico between 1985 and 2009. It also demonstrated that despite underreporting, the rate of decline of murders of men up to 2007 was marked, while the rate of killings of women remained relatively even. Since 2007, homicides generally have been sharply on the increase in the context of insecurity and violence in Mexico. 2010 data not included in the report shows 2,418 murders of women and 23,285 of men—the highest year on record for killings of men and women.

> *Gender-based violence continues to be widespread, with official figures of killings of women rising rapidly in the last three years.*

The report highlights the many flaws that exist in the various procedures for recording and documenting murders of women, which prevent a fuller and more reliable assessment of actual gender-based violence in Mexico and undermine proper investigation of cases, including the routine failure to conduct full autopsies. The report demonstrates that the manner in which official data is gathered makes it impossible to determine the degree to which perpetrators of killings of women are arrested, tried and convicted by the courts. The report concludes that the continuing failure to establish gender sensitive procedures for registering and investigating cases is preventing a fuller and more reliable picture of the pattern of violence against women and levels of impunity emerging.

Despite the limitations, the available data show that killings of women are frequently characterized by direct misogynistic violence:

> "The brutality with which women are murdered is equally demonstrated in the study, which shows that women are three times more likely than men to die by the most cruel means, such as hanging, strangulation, suffocation, drowning, immersion and knives. Women are also three times more likely to be murdered by poisoning or burns with chemicals or fire. In short, a form of dying directly and literally at the hands of the aggressor."

Gender-Based Killings in Chihuahua State

In 2004 the committee concluded an investigation ... into a pattern of gender-based killings and impunity in Ciudad Juárez. Despite the recommendations issued by the committee, and other international and national human rights mechanisms, gender-based killings continue. In Chihuahua state, where there has been a steep rising in the overall homicide rate, one in 14 murder victims were women in 2008 compared with one in 11 in 2010.

In Ciudad Juárez, the killing and abduction of women has reached extremely alarming levels. In 2010, 320 women were killed, according to human rights organizations. In the first three months of 2012, at least 13 bodies of young women and girls were discovered in the Valle de Juárez district outside the city. Seven bodies have reportedly been identified as girls between the ages of 15 and 17 whose abduction from the central district of the city had been reported. Human rights organizations and relatives of victims have reported an increasing number of women abducted and disappeared in recent years.

Amnesty International is concerned that these deaths are not being investigated adequately, facilitating impunity. In March [2012] the state authorities recognised 115 cases of unsolved disappeared women since 1993.

Also in March 2012, the state government made public incorrect information in relation to the work of the Argentine Forensic Anthropology Team (AFAT) which had been invited by federal and state government in 2005 to carry out a forensic project to identify female remains. The state authorities claimed that the international forensic experts had failed to provide full information of remains not identified and that the state only held 30 unidentified bodies of women. In fact as the AFAT pointed out in a letter it made public, they had provided a full report on the 50 remains of women which continued unidentified when the AFAT had concluded its assistance project in Ciudad Juárez in 2010.

In Ciudad Juárez, the killing and abduction of women has reached extremely alarming levels.

The surge in cases of killings and abductions in Ciudad Juárez and the inadequate response of the state authorities strongly suggests that the pattern of gender-based killings and negligence by officials responsible for protection and investigation persists. Human rights organizations in Ciudad Juárez have repeatedly expressed concern to Amnesty International that the high levels of overall violence in recent years in the city have led state and municipal authorities to reassign resources, with the result that there is reduced capacity to register and investigate reports of gender-based abductions and killings.

Insufficient Measures by the Mexican Government

The 2009 judgment by the Inter-American Court of Human Rights on the killing of three young women in Ciudad Juárez

Homicides: Chihuahua State, Mexico			
Year	Men	Women	Total
2008	2,424 (93%)	180 (7%)	2,604
2009	3,457 (94%)	218 (6%)	3,680
2010	5,826 (91%)	584 (9%)	6,421

TAKEN FROM: Amnesty International, "Mexico: Briefing to the UN Committee on the Elimination of Discrimination Against Women," July 2012.

in 2001 found the Mexican state responsible for a series of treaty violations, including discrimination, failure to protect the lives of the victims, failure of due diligence to effectively investigate and failure to hold to account officials responsible. The court ordered the federal, state and municipal authorities to effectively investigate the case; investigate threats and attacks on relatives; improve measures to combat violence against women; establish standard protocols for investigating gender-based crimes; improve emergency coordinated response to reports of missing women (Alba Protocol); establish a DNA database; carry out training and education programmes for police and judges as well as the public; provide medical support and compensation to victims and families.

According to lawyers representing some of the victims, the measures implemented by the government to comply with the judgment have been insufficient. There have been no advances in the investigation into the killing of the young women; public officials have avoided criminal sanctions for their conduct in the original investigations; investigations into threats and attacks against relatives of victims and human rights defenders have produced no results; symbolic acts by the government have been widely criticised by families as ignoring their concerns and the ongoing pattern of gender-based attacks; standardized protocols have been announced but not consulted or reviewed by independent experts and there is not information on their application; the application of the Alba Protocol to search for missing women remains limited to a small proportion of women and girls reported missing each year, severely reducing its impact; information around the establishment of a database on missing women and unidentified female remains is contradictory, with no clear evidence that a reliable database is in operation; there is insufficient information on training and education of public officials responsible for preliminary investigations and judicial proceedings to allow an assessment of their impact on developing gender competence and ending stereotyping; relatives have received compensation ordered by the court but access to ongoing health care needs of victims and to relatives' remains has not been guaranteed.

Periodical and Internet Sources Bibliography

The following articles have been selected to supplement the diverse views presented in this chapter.

Didier Bikorimana	"Rwanda: The Land of Gender Equality?," *Think Africa Press*, May 15, 2012. www.thinkafricapress.com.
Helen Clark	"Family Planning Is a Matter of Social Justice," *New Statesman*, July 11, 2012.
Zuhal Yeşilyurt Gündüz	"Water—On Women's Burdens, Humans' Rights, and Companies' Profits," *Monthly Review*, January 2011.
Louise Hancock and Orzala Ashraf Nemat	"A Place at the Table: Safeguarding Women's Rights in Afghanistan," Oxfam International, October 3, 2011. www.oxfam.org.
Human Rights Watch	"Criminalizing Identities: Rights Abuses in Cameroon Based on Sexual Orientation and Gender Identity," November 2010. www.hrw.org.
Roger Kaplan	"How Not to Promote Freedom in Africa," *American Spectator*, January 17, 2011.
Kathambi Kinoti	"Economic Powerhouse Japan: What About Women's Rights?," Association for Women's Rights in Development, August 26, 2010. www.awid.org.
Simon Montlake	"Gender Inequality Costs Asia $47 Billion Annually," *Christian Science Monitor*, May 9, 2011.
World Bank	"World Development Report 2012: Gender Equality and Development," September 2011.

GLOBALVIEWPOINTS

| Global Social Justice

Debt in Poor Countries Is Unjust and Exploitative

Jubilee Debt Campaign

In the following viewpoint, Jubilee Debt Campaign argues that much of the debt owed to developed countries by poor countries is unjust or illegitimate. The author contends that debt in poor countries is one of the main barriers to development. The author further claims that cancelling much of this debt would save lives and should be done without onerous conditions that enslave poor countries to rich countries. Jubilee Debt Campaign is an organization that calls for cancellation of unjust debt held by poor countries.

As you read, consider the following questions:

1. According to the author, what percentage of developing country debt can be attributed to loans made to dictators?

2. How much debt in poor countries has already been cancelled, according to Jubilee Debt Campaign?

3. How many years, on average, does it take for a country to receive final debt cancellation under the current debt relief schemes, according to the author?

When money is loaned to poorer countries for development it should be done on fair terms and in a responsible way that leads to improved livelihoods and opportunities for the millions who are trapped in the poverty cycle.

Unjust and Illegitimate Debt

Hindsight has revealed many cases of developed countries knowingly loaning billions to corrupt governments in poor countries in order to buy their political allegiance, or profit from loans for obviously useless or overpriced development projects that could never have benefited the populace who wound up paying for them.

Some debts were even run up by the previous colonial regimes and then passed on to newly liberated countries—they were born into debt. Thus, a large proportion of poor country debt is unjust or illegitimate.

Perhaps most unjust and shocking of all, loans were made to regimes and officials who were known to be oppressive or corrupt, such as Saddam Hussein in Iraq who was lent money by the West and Arab states up until the 1991 Gulf War. During the Cold War [the nonviolent conflict between the United States and the former Soviet Union, from 1947–1991] in particular, many dictatorial and corrupt governments had no problem obtaining loans, as long as they proclaimed themselves to be anti-Communist.

Billions have been siphoned off to fund the lavish lifestyles of a few elites, or worse, to purchase arms used to oppress the very people the money was meant to benefit. Long after these nations have rid themselves of corrupt leaders their legacy lives on in the form of massive debts. Of the current total developing country debt, rough estimates suggest some 20%—$500 billion—can be attributed to dictators such as Suharto in Indonesia and [Ferdinand] Marcos in the Philippines.

Debt Costs Lives

Debt is one of the main barriers to development in southern countries today. When poor country governments service huge debt burdens, they often do so with funds urgently needed to provide basic medical care for their citizens and essential services such as clean drinking water. This costs lives.

UNICEF [the United Nations Children's Fund] estimates that almost 10 million children under the age of five die each year from preventable diseases or from drinking polluted water that could be made safe, whilst 1,400 women die in pregnancy or childbirth every day.

A large proportion of poor country debt is unjust or illegitimate.

Meanwhile, many of the poorest countries spend more servicing external debts than on their total health budget. If poor countries spent money on medicines, clean water and schools instead of repaying debts to the rich world, millions of lives could be saved.

According to the Universal Declaration of Human Rights, everyone should enjoy the right to free education, adequate food, housing, and access to medical care and other social services. Governments of indebted nations should not be forced to violate these rights and risk the lives of their citizens in order to service debts owed to rich countries. Such debt is unpayable and should be written off.

Perhaps the most persuasive argument for cancelling third world debt is that it saves lives. According to the World Bank, countries that received multilateral debt cancellation increased their social spending by an average of 45% between 1999 and 2003, meaning that funds for essential services like health care and education increased dramatically. This enables people to escape the downward spiral of poverty and disease, improves opportunities and reduces inequality. . . .

The Campaign to Cancel Debt

Some debt has been cancelled, largely in response to the tireless efforts of debt campaigners around the world.... But it is only a small proportion of the overall debt—around $100 billion—and it's estimated an additional $400 billion of debt cancellation is necessary if 100 countries are to meet their people's basic needs.

It should be pointed out that people campaigning for debt cancellation are not demanding that *all debt everywhere* be cancelled, nor are they suggesting an end to all borrowing and lending.

There may well be good reasons for countries to borrow, for example: to invest in the creation of industry and the development of local businesses, or to provide infrastructure. But lending must be done in a just and responsible way. What campaigners are calling for is an end to unjust, or 'illegitimate,' debt, which should not be paid either because payment is an intolerable burden on poor countries, or because the supposed 'debt' itself is simply unfair.

Most debt relief is delivered through two institutions, the International Monetary Fund (IMF) and the World Bank, both of which are controlled by wealthy creditor nations. They set the rules that allow poor countries to qualify for debt cancellation; if countries do not follow the demands of the IMF and World Bank they cannot get debt relief. On top of this, many countries with unpayable debts do not 'qualify' for debt cancellation at all, often for arbitrary reasons.

The Debt Relief Obstacle Course

All of the debt relief schemes invented to date have done little to challenge the power of the creditors. In fact, in order to obtain their debt relief, countries have to implement a large number of economic conditions that are dictated by the World Bank and IMF.

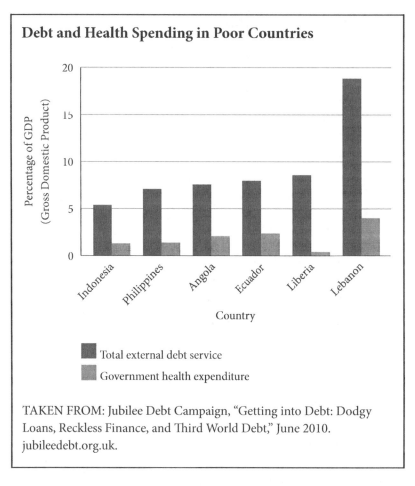

Debt and Health Spending in Poor Countries

TAKEN FROM: Jubilee Debt Campaign, "Getting into Debt: Dodgy Loans, Reckless Finance, and Third World Debt," June 2010. jubileedebt.org.uk.

They are so strict and difficult to fulfill that the process has been referred to as a 'debt relief obstacle course.' Based on a controversial and widely discredited economic dogma known as neoliberalism or the 'Washington Consensus,' these conditions require countries to:

Restrict public expenditure

Governments must spend less on essential services like health care and education, regardless of the needs of their people. All across the developing world, schools and hospitals have had to close or introduce fees because of IMF conditions, denying access to basic medical care and education to those who need it most.

Open up their markets

This means rich international companies from the developed West are able to 'compete' with poor local producers. As if this wasn't already unfair enough, because wealthy nations dictate the trade rules, they maintain all the subsidies (financial support) that protect their industries and producers, while demanding that poor country governments remove all of theirs. This floods poor nations' markets with cheap imports and forces local producers (like farmers) out of business, which leads to unemployment and further poverty. Meanwhile, the already rich Western companies make money out of the poor in developing countries by selling them foodstuffs and goods shipped from across the globe that could have easily been produced locally and benefited the local economy.

All of the debt relief schemes invented to date have done little to challenge the power of creditors.

Privatise their industries

Governments must hand over the running of services like water and electricity to private companies under the assumption that they will run them more efficiently and invest in infrastructure, leading to lower prices and improved service. In reality, it just means that profits come first, and all too often privatisation has resulted in massive price increases with no improvement in service or provision. In fact, in the case of water supply, it has led to people being disconnected because they could no longer afford to pay their bills, forcing them to either walk miles to access another source or drink polluted water.

The Problem with Current Debt Relief

These conditions have been shown time and again to have disastrous effects when imposed on very poor countries. Even if they were good for the country's economy, they are bad for democracy. They mean that the World Bank and IMF have more influence over the country's government than ordinary people in that country do. This removes power from the government and makes it more difficult for ordinary people to hold their leaders to account. Often governments will be going against the will of their people when implementing unpopular economic policies, and must behave in undemocratic ways in order to enforce them.

In addition to undermining democracy, imposing such conditions has also been shown to

- undermine the ability of governments to develop policies in the public interest because the interests of the private sector and lenders must come first.

- lead to civil unrest: public anger at health and education cutbacks has led to anti-IMF riots in a number of countries including Zambia and Nigeria.

- accelerate the depletion of forests, fisheries and minerals by demanding greater levels of exports.

- enhance legal rights that protect foreign investors at the expense of human rights and social reform.

- hinder the fight against HIV/AIDS.

Those countries that decide they will put up with the conditions imposed on them will find it takes on average 3.8 years to receive final debt cancellation—a long time for people who are dying because their governments cannot provide basic health care. Economist Professor Jeffrey Sachs of the United Nations Millennium Project has described IMF and World Bank policies as *"belt tightening for people who cannot afford belts."*

Meanwhile, the wealthy nations who impose these conditions on other countries have yet to submit their own economies to them. In many cases they actually do the opposite to what the IMF prescribes by subsiding their industries, supporting trade protection and minimum wage laws and maintaining spending on public services.

What this adds up to is a pattern of dominance and exploitation that concentrates wealth and power in the north and further impoverishes the south.

So onerous are the conditions attached to debt relief that some nations that qualified for HIPC [heavily indebted poor countries], such as Laos and Sri Lanka, chose not to take part, feeling the conditions and stigma associated with the initiative far outweighed the benefits they might receive.

Indebtedness and Slavery

Many argue that by offering only to reduce debts to a 'sustainable' level, instead of cancelling them outright with no conditions attached, debt relief schemes actually deepen dependency on foreign aid and perpetuate a cycle of borrowing that rich nations profit from.

Many people in debtor countries believe that creditor countries are deliberately keeping them indebted to maintain power over them. Forcing poor country governments to prioritise debt repayments and implement unpopular and harmful social and economic reforms in order to qualify for relief denies them the autonomy to make decisions on the key policies that shape their country, while enabling creditor nations to dictate whatever policies and trade rules serve them best.

What this adds up to is a pattern of dominance and exploitation that concentrates wealth and power in the north and further impoverishes the south. It's a pattern that has been repeated throughout the history of the debt crisis and has led many people to compare indebtedness to slavery.

Rich Countries Must Do More than Poor Countries to Fight Climate Change

José Antonio Ocampo and Nicholas Stern

In the following viewpoint, José Antonio Ocampo and Nicholas Stern argue that rich countries need to take the lead in investing in sustainable growth to avert climate change. The authors contend that rich nations cannot expect the developing world to halt development and growth, and they call on developed countries to accelerate their actions. Ocampo is a professor in the School of International and Public Affairs at Columbia University in New York City. Stern is I.G. Patel Professor of Economics and Government and chair of the Grantham Research Institute on Climate Change and the Environment at the London School of Economics and Political Science.

As you read, consider the following questions:

1. The authors contend that the world is headed for how much of a global warming by 2020?

2. The developing world will be home to how many of the projected global population of nine billion in 2050, according to the authors?

3. What do the authors say is the answer to combating climate change?

As the United Nations [UN] conference on sustainable development begins [June 20, 2012] it is the rich countries that have the most to prove. The last summit in Rio de Janeiro 20 years ago provided the opportunity for countries to sign the UN framework convention on climate change, which should have stabilised global annual emissions of greenhouse gases at 1990 levels, and placed prime responsibility on the industrialised nations, who have done most to pollute the atmosphere, to lead by example.

The Failure of Rich Countries to Lead

But rich countries have not led and annual global emissions have continued to rise. Even taking into account pledges by rich and poor nations for action by 2020, the world appears to be heading for likely global warming of 3°C [approximately 6°F] or more, to a temperature not seen on earth for about 3m [3 million] years.

Having witnessed, for instance, failure by the US and Canada to honour their signatures to the Kyoto Protocol [an international agreement aimed at reducing greenhouse gas emissions], poor countries are understandably sceptical, as we approach another summit, of lofty ambitions expressed by rich nations.

> *Rich countries have not led and annual global emissions have continued to rise.*

It will take more than words to restore the confidence of poor countries. Some rich countries are dragging their feet on tackling climate change while unfairly criticising the developing world, apparently unaware of the strides that these countries are making in finding a new path. China, India, Mexico, Brazil and other emerging powers have laid out ambitious plans to tackle deforestation and to reduce radically their emissions to output ratios. Most importantly, they are implementing those plans.

The Challenge for Poor Countries

One of the biggest injustices of climate change is that the poorest countries are most exposed and vulnerable to the impacts of climate change even though they have done least to raise atmospheric levels of greenhouse gases. Now they must contend with the brutal arithmetic of a tight budget for global emissions as they try to fight poverty, develop and grow, while managing the enormous risks of climate change.

Rich and poor countries agreed in Cancún in December 2010 that global emissions should be reduced to avoid a rise in global average temperatures of over 2°C. To have a reasonable chance of this, global average emissions have to be reduced from the present level of about 7 tonnes per capita of carbon dioxide equivalent to around 2 tonnes in 2050.

Some rich countries are dragging their feet on tackling climate change while unfairly criticising the developing world.

This is a huge challenge as developing countries will be home to 8bn [8 billion] of the projected global population in 2050 of 9bn. Even if the rich countries reduce their emissions to zero by 2030, developing nations would need to hold their emissions to about 5 tonnes per capita by 2030 and 2.5 tonnes by 2050. For comparison, current per capita emissions are 22 tonnes in the US, over 9 tonnes in the EU [European Union], about 7 tonnes in China, and 2 tonnes in India.

A Sustainable Path for the Future

So rich countries not only have to accelerate their actions, but must also support the poor countries as they make the transition to low-carbon economic growth.

Adaptation to Climate Change

Climate change is a reality. Action is needed now to help the world's poorest people cope in the face of a changing climate.

Unwittingly over the past century, the industrialised world sowed the seeds of disaster by burning fossil fuels. Today, the world's poor are paying the price. Wealthier nations have a moral responsibility to pay for the damage that climate change is now creating and to support the costs of adaptation in developing countries.

"Stop Climate Injustice:
Climate Change Is Killing the Developing World,"
Practical Action, www.practicalaction.org.

It would be morally unacceptable to try to insist that developing countries drop or scale back plans to fight poverty and raise material standards of living. The developing world is understandably suspicious that this is a hidden agenda. Yet it is a fact that their growth is the biggest source of the rise of emissions. The answer is clear: radical change in emissions per unit of output. This revolution carries many benefits: cleaner, quieter, safer, more energy-secure, and more biologically diverse energy. Rich countries must support this with technology and resources.

Rich countries not only have to accelerate their actions, but must also support the poor countries as they make the transition to low-carbon economic growth.

The developed world must not attempt to preach to the poorer nations. As they deal with the largely self-inflicted damage to their economies, rich countries must show they understand the dangers that arise from hesitation in acting against climate change. They will discover by investing in the low-carbon economy, adopting clear and credible policies, and building new technologies and markets [that] they will help to create the only truly sustainable growth path for the future, and help find a way out of the depression of their own making.

The Food Crisis in the Developing World Is Unfair and Unjust

Jim Goodman

In the following viewpoint, Jim Goodman argues that the solution to hunger in the developing world will not be solved by high-technology agriculture. Goodman claims that the food crisis is not an issue of food shortage but rather an inability to get food to those who need it. Goodman contends that poor agricultural policy is ultimately the problem, and the solution is traditional agriculture. Goodman is a farmer and farm activist advocating for a farmer-controlled consumer-oriented food system.

As you read, consider the following questions:

1. The author suggests that what four factors contribute to hunger in the world?
2. The increased wheat prices that caused food riots in Mozambique, according to Goodman, were caused by what?
3. The author claims that the function of industrial agriculture—in contrast to the function of a just farming system—is to do what?

The food crisis of 2008 never really ended; it was ignored and forgotten. The rich and powerful are well fed; they had no food crisis, no shortage, so in the West, it was little more than a short-lived sound bite, tragic but forgettable. To the poor in the developing world, whose ability to afford food is no better now than in 2008, the hunger continues.

The Proposed High-Technology Solution to Hunger

Hunger can have many contributing factors: natural disaster, discrimination, war, poor infrastructure. So why, regardless of the situation, is high-tech agriculture always assumed to be the only solution? This premise is put forward and supported by those who would benefit financially if their "solution" were implemented. Corporations peddle their high-technology genetically engineered seed and chemical packages, their genetically altered animals, always with the "promise" of feeding the world.

Politicians and philanthropists, who may mean well, jump on the high-technology band wagon. Could the promise of financial support or investment return fuel their apparent compassion?

The Alliance for a Green Revolution in Africa (AGRA), an initiative of the Bill and Melinda Gates Foundation and the Rockefeller Foundation, supposedly works to achieve a food secure and prosperous Africa. While these sentiments and goals may be philanthropy at its best, some of the coalition partners have a different agenda.

Shortages occur because of the inability to get food where it is needed and the inability of the hungry to afford it.

One of the key players in AGRA, Monsanto, hopes to spread its genetically engineered seed throughout Africa by promising better yields, drought resistance, an end to hunger, etc. Could a new green revolution succeed where the original green revolution had failed? Or was the whole concept of a green revolution a pig in a poke to begin with?

Monsanto giving free seed to poor small holder farmers sounds great, or are they just setting the hook? Remember, next year those farmers will have to buy their seed. Interesting to note that the Gates Foundation purchased $23.1 million worth of Monsanto stock in the second quarter of 2010. Do they also see the food crisis in Africa as a potential to turn a nice profit? Every corporation has one overriding interest—self-interest, but surely not charitable foundations?

The Causes of Food Shortages

Food shortages are seldom about a lack of food; there is plenty of food in the world. The shortages occur because of the inability to get food where it is needed and the inability of the hungry to afford it. These two problems are principally caused by, as Frances Moore Lappé put it, a lack of justice. There are also ethical considerations; a higher value should be placed on people than on corporate profit. This must be at the forefront, not an afterthought.

In 2008, there were shortages of food, in some places, for some people. There was never a shortage of food in 2008 on a global basis, nor is there currently. True, some countries, in Africa for example, do not have enough food where it is needed, yet people with money have their fill no matter where they live. Poverty and inequality cause hunger.

The current [2010] food riots in Mozambique were a result of increased wheat prices on the world market. The UN [United Nations] Food and Agriculture Organization (FAO) estimates the world is on course to the third largest wheat harvest in history, so increasing wheat prices were not caused by actual shortages, but rather by speculation on the price of wheat in the international market.

While millions of people go hungry in India, thousands of kilos of grain rot in storage. Unable to afford the grain, the hungry depend on the government to distribute food. Apparently that's not going so well.

Hunger and Agricultural Policy

Not everyone living in a poor country goes hungry; those with money eat. Not everyone living in a rich country is well fed; those without money go hungry. We in the US are said to have the safest and most abundant food supply in the world, yet even here, surrounded by an overabundance of food, there are plenty of hungry people and their numbers are growing. Do we too have a food crisis, concurrent with an obesity crisis?

Why is there widespread hunger? Is food a right? Is profit taking through speculation that drives food prices out of the reach of the poor a right? Is pushing high-technology agriculture on an entire continent that could feed itself a (corporate) right?

In developing countries, those with hunger and poor food distribution, the small farmers, most of whom are women, have little say in agricultural policy. The framework of international trade and the rules imposed by the International Monetary Fund and World Bank on developing countries places emphasis on crops for export, not crops for feeding a hungry population.

A new green revolution based on genetically engineered crops, imported fertilizer and government-imposed agricultural policy will not feed the world.

Despite what we hope are the best intentions of the Gates Foundation, a new green revolution based on genetically engineered crops, imported fertilizer and government-imposed agricultural policy will not feed the world. Women, not Monsanto, feed most of the world's population, and the greatest portion of the world's diet still relies on crops and farming systems developed and cultivated by the indigenous for centuries, systems that still work, systems that offer real promise.

The Best Hope for Ending Hunger

The report of 400 experts from around the world, the International Assessment of Agricultural [Knowledge,] Science and Technology for Development (IAASTD), is ignored by the proponents of a new green revolution, precisely because it shows that the best hope for ending hunger lies with local, traditional, farmer-controlled agricultural production, not high-tech industrial agriculture.

To feed the world, fair methods of land distribution must be considered. A fair and just food system depends on small holder farmers having access to land. The function of a just farming system is to insure that everyone gets to eat; industrial agriculture functions to insure those corporations controlling the system make a profit.

The ultimate cause of hunger is not a lack of Western ag-ricultural technology, rather hunger results when people are not allowed to participate in a food system of their choosing. Civil wars, structural adjustment policies, inadequate distribu-tion systems, international commodity speculation and corpo-rate control of food from seed to table—these are the causes of hunger, the stimulus for food crises.

If the Gates Foundation is serious about ending hunger in Africa, they need to read the IAASTD report, not Monsanto's quarterly profit report. Then they can decide how their money might best be spent.

Increasing Foreign Aid Not Necessarily Good for Developing Countries

Moses Bosire

In the following viewpoint, Moses Bosire argues that foreign aid is not necessarily beneficial for recipient countries. Bosire claims that foreign aid in Kenya and elsewhere actually helps to prop up the status quo, supporting bad governance. Bosire claims that rather than giving more money to aid that has not been proven to be effective, existing aid should be used to develop a better alternative that will bring about transformational change. Bosire writes a blog called blog.mkenya.org and contributes to Mwakilishi.com.

As you read, consider the following questions:

1. According to Bosire, how does foreign aid distort the system?

2. The author suggests that the quality of existing foreign aid should be improved by ensuring that aid does what?

3. Rather than an emphasis on boosting incomes, Bosire claims that donor-funded development initiatives should have an emphasis on what?

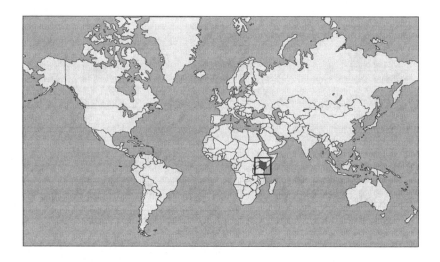

Greed knows no bounds. The predatory political system in Kenya personifies this idiom in the way it continues to facilitate massive looting of public coffers by a few corrupt individuals with little regard for the impoverished masses who continue to be ravaged by wanton poverty because the money that was supposed to provide for their common well-being is sitting in the pockets or bank accounts of a few individuals.

This untenable system continues to thrive in many poor countries due to one major factor: foreign aid. The huge inflow of well-intentioned donor funds distorts the system by creating an illusion of normalcy which is not supported by existing social, economic and political conditions.

Despite consuming billions of dollars, the effectiveness of foreign aid in supporting development in poor countries remains a very controversial issue. There is simply no correlation between the huge quantities of cash injections and the impact (or lack of it) on the ground.

Whereas foreign aid creates a lot of activities that make it seem as if something is happening, it remains captive to the same status quo forces that gladly use it as a cover for their mismanagement and misappropriation of public resources.

So although foreign aid is meant to support development, it is inadvertently propping up the status quo and consequently stifling development thus defeating its own purpose. I believe that the conditions that impoverish people in Kenya making them vulnerable to destructive political manipulation and exploitation are the same conditions that hinder the effectiveness of foreign aid as a tool for supporting development.

Therefore the priority should be in addressing these conditions because no matter the quantity of foreign aid, under the same conditions the results are likely to be the same which makes the calls to increase aid to poor countries in order to spur development questionable.

Donor funds that serve to prop up the status quo in poor countries are bad quality, so increasing the quantity of such funds defeats logic. The focus should be on first improving the quality of existing levels of funding by ensuring they are having a visible and measurable impact and not just propping up the status quo.

Although foreign aid is meant to support development, it is inadvertently propping up the status quo and consequently stifling development thus defeating its own purpose.

In order to increase or maximize the effectiveness of foreign aid, the objective must shift from just wanting to alleviate or improve the social, economic and political situation in poor countries and instead focus on transforming the situation. Transformational change means a change that is not merely an extension, continuation or improvement over the past but a shift in mind-set, behaviour and ways of doing things. The rationale of any transformation agenda is to develop a better alternative situation to the status quo.

Traditionally, donor-funded development initiatives have placed more emphasis on boosting the incomes of households

---

Foreign Aid to Africa

Giving alms to Africa remains one of the biggest ideas of our time—millions march for it, governments are judged by it, celebrities proselytize the need for it. Calls for more aid to Africa are growing louder, with advocates pushing for doubling the roughly $50 billion of international assistance that already goes to Africa each year.

Yet evidence overwhelmingly demonstrates that aid to Africa has made the poor poorer, and the growth slower. The insidious aid culture has left African countries more debt laden, more inflation prone, more vulnerable to the vagaries of the currency markets and more unattractive to higher quality investment. It's increased the risk of civil conflict and unrest. Aid is an unmitigated political, economic and humanitarian disaster.

Dambisa Moyo, "Why Foreign Aid Is Hurting Africa,"
Wall Street Journal, *March 21, 2009.*

---

or individuals with the aim of reducing the number of people living on less than a dollar a day. But if the objective is transformational change, then there should be as much, if not more, emphasis on safeguarding the human dignity of communities.

Improving the quality rather than increasing the quantity of aid should be the priority.

The assumption is that protecting and promoting the human dignity of communities will drive transformational change which will empower people and consequently create the conducive environment required for more effective development initiatives.

For instance, facilitating access to dignified public/ community services for the poor majority will help create a compelling precedent that could allow people the opportunity to experience, hence expect and demand, better services. This would drive transformational change in terms of raising expectations for better governance and prudent management of public resources, hence addressing one of the root causes of poverty in Africa—i.e., bad governance.

Despite being critical of the negative unintended impacts of foreign aid in developing countries, I believe aid still has a huge role to play in supporting development efforts in poor countries. However, improving the quality rather than increasing the quantity of aid should be the priority.

Foreign Aid from the United Kingdom to India Is Unnecessary

Nick Wood

In the following viewpoint, Nick Wood argues that the United Kingdom is spending too much money on foreign aid. Wood claims that aid given to India makes no sense with India's economy booming and more billionaires in India than in Great Britain. Wood says that the Indian government itself does not want the aid and, thus, the aid should be cut and the money used domestically. Wood is a columnist for the Daily Mail *in the United Kingdom.*

As you read, consider the following questions:

1. How much money does the United Kingdom spend each year on foreign aid, according to Wood?

2. Wood claims that the police budget in Britain has been cut by what percentage?

3. What fraction of the world's poor lives in India, according to the author?

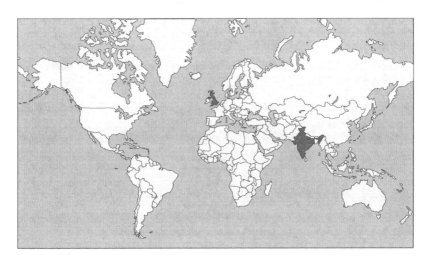

No good deed ever goes unpunished. That must be the thought flitting through the mind of International Development Secretary Andrew Mitchell as he contemplates Sunday's [February 5, 2012] front pages: "India tells Britain—We don't want your aid."

Foreign Aid from the United Kingdom

Most people find it staggering that in the midst of the biggest spending cutbacks since the 1930s, Britain is not only maintaining its foreign aid budget—it is increasing it.

We are currently spending about £9 billion [approx $14.5 billion] a year and under our commitment to increase total aid spending to the UN [United Nations] target of 0.7 per cent of GDP [gross domestic product] by 2013, we are on course for about £12 billion by 2014.

As a percentage of GDP, the UK [United Kingdom] spends more on aid than any of the G8 group of large and wealthy countries.

More and more people also find it staggering that we are giving India another £600 million over the next three years and have already given them £1 billion over the last five years.

After all, the Indian economy is growing at 10 per cent per annum and is set to overtake the UK's in total size within a decade. India has nuclear weapons and a space programme. It has more billionaires than Britain. Its giant £83 billion industrial conglomerate Tata (made up of over 100 companies worldwide) actually owns the iconic British car firm Jaguar Land Rover and what is left of our steel industry.

As a percentage of GDP, the UK spends more on aid than any of the G8 group of large and wealthy countries.

So why are we giving them money? Shouldn't it be the other way round?

Controversial Aid to India

Certainly, the Indians seem to think that the days of the Raj [British Empire in India] and British paternalism are gone.

As Pranab Mukherjee, the Indian finance minister, told the Indian Parliament last week: "We do not require the aid. It is a peanut in our total development exercises." Delhi wanted voluntarily to give it up.

But the British would not let him. According to the *Sunday Telegraph*, officials in our Department for International Development (DFID) told the Indians that cancelling the aid programme would cause "grave political embarrassment" to Britain.

The officials added that ministers such as Mitchell and David Cameron had spent political capital justifying Indian aid to the British people.

This sounds like something out of *Alice in Wonderland*. A cash-strapped Western country, forced to slash its police budget by 20 per cent, close libraries, sack [lay off] soldiers and get rid of its aircraft carriers and Harrier jump jets, is giving money to an emerging Asian superpower. And the superpower does not even want the cash on the grounds that handouts damage its image.

Nor has our largesse bought us influence. In a spectacular slap in the face, India has chosen the "Asda" [basic] option, placing a provisional £6.3 billion contract for fighter jets with the French, rather than the "Waitrose" [upscale] choice of our superior Typhoon planes. . . .

The Need to Cut Aid

Some sense has been injected into the DFID budget. Aid to China and Russia has been stopped and Mitchell can argue that with a third of the world's poorest people (450 million) living in India on about 80p [approximately $1.30] a day, we should be giving them help.

India's plea—to keep our aid money for ourselves, or those who need it more—should be heeded.

But there are poor people in every country, even the United States. And no one is suggesting that we start giving aid to California, even if some of them are having a rough time. Barring extremes like an earthquake or a tsunami, the poor people of countries like the USA or India are fundamentally the responsibility of the domestic government. India could cut back on some of its more grandiose schemes, like their nukes or their space programme, if they wanted to help their own poor.

Under Labour [previous government] Britain was giving aid to about 100 countries, nearly half the world. Sensibly, this has been cut back and aid is better targeted on the poorest and those most in need.

But India's plea—to keep our aid money for ourselves, or those who need it more—should be heeded in Whitehall [the site of main government offices in Britain]. Most of us don't want to fork out extra cash so Dave and Co can feel better about themselves.

Periodical and Internet Sources Bibliography

The following articles have been selected to supplement the diverse views presented in this chapter.

Gordon Brown	"A Plan to Teach the World," *New Statesman*, June 15, 2011.
Bo Ekman	"Interconnectedness Dooms Nations and Their Arbitrary Borders," *Epoch Times*, June 5, 2011. www.theepochtimes.com.
James Ensor	"Deep Injustice at the Heart of Climate Change," ABC (Australian Broadcasting Corporation), June 11, 2009. www.abc.net.au.
Fairtrade Foundation	"The Great Cotton Stitch-Up," November 2010. www.fairtrade.org.uk.
Kevin Gallagher	"The Developing World Is Too Big to Fail," *Guardian* (UK), March 5, 2009.
Ian Gough	"Climate Change, Double Injustice, and Social Policy: A Case Study of the United Kingdom," United Nations Research Institute for Sustainable Development, 2011. www.unrisd.org.
Martin Hickman	"West's Billions in Subsidy Shut Out African Cotton Growers," *Independent* (UK), November 15, 2010.
John Hilary	"The Perils of More Globalization," *Guardian* (UK), February 3, 2009.
Gideon Polya	"Climate Censorship and Climate Injustice," Countercurrents.org, July 4, 2011.
Sam Wong	"EU's 'Renewable Revolution'—Does It Create More Energy Injustice in Developing Countries?," *Journal of Earth Science and Climate Change*, vol. 3, no. 1, 2012.

For Further Discussion

Chapter 1

1. Joseph E. Stiglitz asserts that the middle class in America is doing worse economically than a decade ago. What reasons does Stiglitz give for this, and to what does he think the consequences of such inequality will lead?

2. Several authors in this chapter discuss the impact that growth has had on inequality in various regions of the world. What is one criticism of growth policies that comes up repeatedly? Provide examples from the viewpoints to support your answer.

Chapter 2

1. Based on what Mitsuharu Vincent Okada says about Japan's official recognition of the Ainu people, do you think this provides reason to dispute the viewpoint of Australia's Aboriginal and Torres Strait Islander Social Justice Commissioner that constitutional recognition of indigenous peoples would have a symbolic and practical impact? Explain your reasoning.

Chapter 3

1. In the viewpoints of both Ana Revenga and Sudhir Shetty and the Organisation for Economic Co-operation and Development (OECD), statistics about differences between men and women are cited in support of the claim that gender inequality exists. Do all differences mean that discrimination exists? Why or why not?

2. Assessing the viewpoints in this chapter, what are the top barriers to gender equality around the world? Explain.

Chapter 4

1. Drawing on the various viewpoints in this chapter, do you think that richer countries have an obligation to help poorer countries? Why or why not? Provide examples from the viewpoints to support your answer.

Organizations to Contact

The editors have compiled the following list of organizations concerned with the issues debated in this book. The descriptions are derived from materials provided by the organizations. All have publications or information available for interested readers. The list was compiled on the date of publication of the present volume; the information provided here may change. Be aware that many organizations take several weeks or longer to respond to inquiries, so allow as much time as possible.

African Commission on Human and Peoples' Rights
31 Bijilo Annex Layout, Kombo North District
Western Region, PO Box 673, Banjul
    The Gambia
(220) 441 05 05 • fax: (220) 441 05 04
e-mail: au-banjul@africa-union.org
website: www.achpr.org

The African Commission on Human and Peoples' Rights interprets the African Charter on Human and Peoples' Rights, aiming to promote and protect the rights of Africans. The commission undertakes studies and research on African human rights; organizes seminars, symposia, and conferences; disseminates information; and makes recommendations to African governments. Available at its website is the text of the African Charter on Human and Peoples' Rights.

Amnesty International
1 Easton Street, London   WC1X 0DW
    United Kingdom
(44) 20 7413 5500 • fax: (44) 20 7956 1157
website: www.amnesty.org

Amnesty International is a worldwide movement of people who campaign for internationally recognized human rights for all. Amnesty International conducts research and generates action to prevent and end grave abuses of human rights and to demand justice for those whose rights have been violated. At its website, Amnesty International has numerous publications on a variety of social justice issues.

Association for Women's Rights in Development (AWID)

215 Spadina Avenue, Suite 150, Toronto, Ontario M5T 2C7
  Canada
(416) 594-3773 • fax: (416) 594-0330
e-mail: contact@awid.org
website: www.awid.org

The Association for Women's Rights in Development (AWID) is an international membership organization committed to achieving gender equality, sustainable development, and women's rights. AWID aims to strengthen the voice, impact, and influence of women's rights advocates, organizations, and movements internationally to effectively advance the rights of women. AWID has a variety of reports and briefs available at its website, including "Achieving Women's Economic and Social Rights: Strategies and Lessons from Experience."

Centre for Economic Policy Research (CEPR)

53–56 Great Sutton Street, London EC1V 0DG
  United Kingdom
(44) 20 7183 8801 • fax: (44) 20 7183 8820
e-mail: cepr@cepr.org
website: www.cepr.org

The Centre for Economic Policy Research (CEPR) is the leading European research network in economics. CEPR gathers data through a network of academic researches and disseminates the results to the private sector and policy community. CEPR produces a wide range of reports, books, and conference volumes each year, including "Global Imbalances and the Paradox of Thrift."

Economic Policy Institute (EPI)

1333 H Street NW, Suite 300, East Tower
Washington, DC 20005-4707

(202) 775-8810 • fax: (202) 775-0819
e-mail: epi@epi.org
website: www.epi.org

The Economic Policy Institute (EPI) is a nonprofit think tank that seeks to broaden the discussion about economic policy to include the interests of low- and middle-income workers. EPI briefs policy makers at all levels of government; provides technical support to national, state, and local activists and community organizations; testifies before national, state, and local legislatures; and provides information and background to the print and electronic media. EPI publishes books, studies, issue briefs, popular education materials, and other publications, among which is the biennially published *State of Working America.*

Global Health Council

c/o Global Impact, 66 Canal Center Plaza, Suite 310
Alexandria, VA 22314
website: www.globalhealth.org

The Global Health Council is a nonprofit membership organization dedicated to improving the health of the two billion people who live on less than $2 a day. The Global Health Council implements programs, delivers health care services, conducts research on key issues, advocates for improved policies and financial support, provides funding for global health programming, and develops lifesaving products. The Global Health Council publishes *Global Health* magazine, policy briefs, and fact sheets.

Global Policy Forum (GPF) Europe

Koenigstrasse 37a, Bonn D-53115
  Germany
(49) 228 965 0510 • fax: (49) 228 963 8206
e-mail: europe@globalpolicy.org
website: www.globalpolicy.org/gpf-europe

Global Policy Forum (GPF) Europe is a nonprofit organization, with consultative status at the United Nations (UN). The mission of GPF Europe is to monitor European policy making at the UN, promote accountability of global decisions, educate and mobilize for global citizen participation, and advocate on vital issues of international peace and justice. GPF Europe publishes policy papers, articles, and statements, including the briefing paper "Thinking Ahead: Development Models and Indicators of Well-Being Beyond the MDGs."

Human Rights Watch (HRW)
350 Fifth Avenue, 34th Floor, New York, NY   10118-3299
(212) 290-4700 • fax: (212) 736-1300
e-mail: hrwnyc@hrw.org
website: www.hrw.org

Human Rights Watch (HRW) is dedicated to protecting the human rights of people around the world. HRW investigates human rights abuses, educates the public, and works to change policy and practice. HRW publishes the annual "World Report" and numerous reports, including "Hate on the Streets: Xenophobic Violence in Greece."

Institute of Development Studies (IDS)
Library Road, Brighton   BN1 9RE
    United Kingdom
(44) 1273 606261 • fax: (44) 1273 621202
e-mail: ids@ids.ac.uk
website: www.ids.ac.uk

The Institute of Development Studies (IDS) is a global charity for international development research, teaching, and communications. IDS hosts six research teams, eight postgraduate courses, and offers knowledge services. IDS publishes the *IDS Bulletin* six times a year as well as periodic policy briefings and research reports.

International Monetary Fund (IMF)
700 Nineteenth Street NW, Washington, DC   20431
(202) 623-7000 • fax: (202) 623-4661
e-mail: publicaffairs@imf.org
website: www.imf.org

The International Monetary Fund (IMF) is an organization of 186 countries working to foster global monetary cooperation, secure financial stability, facilitate international trade, promote high employment and sustainable economic growth, and reduce poverty around the world. The IMF monitors the world's economies, lends to members in economic difficulty, and provides technical assistance. The IMF publishes fact sheets, reports on key issues, and the "IMF Annual Report."

Organisation for Economic Co-operation and Development (OECD)

2, rue André Pascal, Paris Cedex 16   75775
  France
(33) 45 24 82 00 • fax: (33) 45 24 85 00
website: www.oecd.org

The Organisation for Economic Co-operation and Development (OECD) works to improve the economic and social well-being of people around the world. The OECD is a membership organization of thirty-four advanced and emerging countries around the world that work to foster prosperity worldwide. The OECD publishes economic surveys and health policy studies about individual nations and studies comparing nations, including numerous studies within its Society at a Glance series.

Oxfam International

Suite 20, 266 Banbury Road, Oxford   OX2 7DL
  United Kingdom
(44) 1865 339 100 • fax: (44) 1865 339 101
e-mail: information@oxfaminternational.org
website: www.oxfam.org

Oxfam International is a confederation of organizations working to end poverty and injustice. Oxfam works to create programs to eradicate poverty and combat injustice, delivers life-saving assistance to people affected by natural disasters and conflict, and aims to raise public awareness of the causes of poverty. Oxfam publishes numerous research and analysis, available at its website, such as "Living on a Spike: How Is the 2011 Food Price Crisis Affecting Poor People?"

Society for International Development (SID)

Via Ardeatina 802, Rome   00178
  Italy
(39) 64872172 • fax: (39) 64872170
website: www.sidint.net

The Society for International Development (SID) is a global network of individuals and institutions concerned with development that is participative, pluralistic, and sustainable. SID aims to facilitate dialogue and help build consensus between various stakeholders and interest groups through its programs and initiatives. SID publishes several reports, including "The State of East Africa 2012: Deepening Integration, Intensifying Challenges."

United Nations (UN)

One United Nations Plaza, New York, NY   10017
(212) 906-5000 • fax: (212) 906-5001
website: www.un.org

The United Nations (UN) is an international organization of 193 member states committed to maintaining international peace and security; developing friendly relations among nations; and promoting social progress, better living standards, and human rights. The UN works around the world in peacekeeping, peace building, conflict prevention, and humanitarian assistance. The UN publishes numerous annual human development reports and other publications, which are available at its website.

World Bank

1818 H Street NW, Washington, DC   20433
(202) 473-1000 • fax: (202) 477-6391
website: www.worldbank.org

The World Bank is made up of two unique development institutions owned by 187 member countries: the International Bank for Reconstruction and Development (IBRD) and the International Development Association (IDA). The World Bank provides low-interest loans, interest-free credits, and grants to developing countries for a wide array of purposes. The World Bank publishes the annual World Development Report and World Development Indicators.

Bibliography of Books

Ayelet Banai, Miriam Ronzoni, and Christian Schemmel, eds.   *Social Justice, Global Dynamics: Theoretical and Empirical Perspectives.* New York: Routledge, 2011.

Abhijit V. Banerjee and Esther Duflo   *Poor Economics: A Radical Rethinking of the Way to Fight Global Poverty.* New York: PublicAffairs, 2011.

Günseli Berik, Yana van der Meulen Rodgers, and Ann Zammit, eds.   *Social Justice and Gender Equality: Rethinking Development Strategies and Macroeconomic Policies.* New York: Routledge, 2009.

Alison Brysk   *Global Good Samaritans: Human Rights as Foreign Policy.* New York: Oxford University Press, 2009.

Gary Craig, Tania Burchardt, and David Gordon, eds.   *Social Justice and Public Policy: Seeking Fairness in Diverse Societies.* Bristol, England: Policy Press, 2008.

Olaf Cramme and Patrick Diamond, eds.   *Social Justice in the Global Age.* Malden, MA: Polity, 2009.

Cynthia Gerstl-Pepin and Judith A. Aiken, eds.   *Social Justice Leadership for a Global World.* Charlotte, NC: Information Age Publishing, 2012.

Abigail Gosselin   *Global Poverty and Individual Responsibility.* Lanham, MD: Lexington Books, 2009.

Duncan Green	*From Poverty to Power: How Active Citizens and Effective States Can Change the World.* Oxford: Oxfam International, 2008.
David Harvey	*Social Justice and the City.* Athens: University of Georgia Press, 2009.
David Hulme	*Global Poverty: How Global Governance Is Failing the Poor.* New York: Routledge, 2010.
Dean Karlan and Jacob Appel	*More than Good Intentions: How a New Economics Is Helping to Solve Global Poverty.* New York: Dutton, 2011.
Paul Kriese and Randall E. Osborne	*Social Justice, Poverty and Race: Normative and Empirical Points of View.* New York: Rodopi, 2011.
Luis F. López-Calva and Nora Lustig	*Declining Inequality in Latin America: A Decade of Progress?* Washington, DC: Brookings Institution Press, 2010.
Mark Lusk, Kathleen Staudt, and Eva Moya, eds.	*Social Justice in the U.S.-Mexico Border Region.* New York: Springer, 2012.
Behrooz Morvaridi	*Social Justice and Development.* New York: Palgrave Macmillan, 2008.
Padmini Murthy and Clyde Lanford Smith	*Women's Global Health and Human Rights.* Sudbury, MA: Jones and Bartlett Publishers, 2010.

T.Y. Okosun	*Social Justice and Increasing Global Destitution*. Lanham, MD: University Press of America, 2009.
Anya Schiffrin and Eamon Kircher-Allen, eds.	*From Cairo to Wall Street: Voices from the Global Spring*. New York: New Press, 2012.
Adrian Smith, Alison Stenning, and Katie Willis, eds.	*Social Justice and Neoliberalism: Global Perspectives*. New York: Palgrave Macmillan, 2008.
Ida Susser	*AIDS, Sex, and Culture: Global Politics and Survival in Southern Africa*. Malden, MA: Wiley-Blackwell, 2009.
Laura Valentini	*Justice in a Globalized World: A Normative Framework*. New York: Oxford University Press, 2011.
Jeffrey G. Williamson	*Trade and Poverty: When the Third World Fell Behind*. Cambridge, MA: MIT Press, 2011.

Index

Geographic headings and page numbers in **boldface** refer to viewpoints about that country or region.